Programme Notes

Case studies for locating
experimental theatre
revised and expanded
second edition

Contents

Programme Notes, 2007

Introduction

Lois Keidan and CJ Mitchell

Programme Notes is about furthering dialogues and collaborations across the spectrum of contemporary theatre in the UK.

In 2006, the Live Art Development Agency was commissioned by Arts Council England to undertake research aimed at exploring and fostering new relations between the theatrical 'mainstream' and artists from the independent sector. The project was grounded in the understanding that across the UK venue directors and programmers were increasingly excited by work that pushed at the edges of our expectations of what theatre can be, and that there had perhaps never been a better time to progress the work of independent theatre-makers, or for theatre venues to take a fresh look at what they can do, and how they can do it.

The result of the research was the publication *Programme Notes, Case Studies For Locating Experimental Theatre (2007)*, which featured a series of essays and case studies illustrating the ways in which contemporary theatre was changing and innovating in different contexts, especially in regard to the relationships between established venues and experimental practices and approaches.

Programme Notes reflected the possibilities of a truly forward-looking theatre through the artistic aspirations, new approaches and cultural diversity of its practitioners, as well as providing practical insights into specific projects, programming initiatives and audience development work. The publication featured contributions by Lyn Gardner, Tim

Etchells, Neil Bartlett, Stella Hall, John E McGrath, Alan Rivett, Mark Borkowski, Rose Fenton, Brian Logan, Lucy Neal, Keith Khan, Simon Casson, Louise Jeffreys, Judith Knight and Toni Racklin. *Plays International* wrote, "this small, cutely presented volume may turn out to be the most significant British Theatre book published this year."

Things have changed considerably since 2007, with many more large-scale festivals and venues in the UK now engaging with different ways of creating, presenting and representing new theatre and performance. There has been an increasing move away from the perceived binary opposites of large-scale producers working with huge budgets to produce traditional theatre events and small-scale venues and independent producers working on a shoestring to support experimental work. The theatre landscape in the UK today is a much more complex and interesting ecosystem where large-scale venues and producers are increasingly engaging with experimental practices and talking to new kinds of audiences, and many independent artists and producers are working on large-scale, and dare one say 'popular', events. As we write this introduction the London International Festival of Theatre (LIFT) has just produced a five-week sold out run of Elevator Repair Service's *Gatz* at the Noël Coward Theatre in London's West End.

This expanded edition of *Programme Notes* sets out to reflect some of the key shifts that have taken place since 2007 with four new case studies about the work of the Manchester International Festival, National Theatre of Scotland, BAC (Battersea Arts Centre) and Forest Fringe.

Andy Field and Deborah Pearson have written about their groundbreaking work as Co-Directors of Forest Fringe and the ways they have broken (into) the Edinburgh Festival through the creation of new production models for artists and audiences alike.

David Jubb and David Micklem, joint Artistic Directors of BAC, have written an ABC of BAC, expanding on the many ways they are working to invent the future of theatre.

Vicky Featherstone, Artistic Director of the National Theatre of Scotland (NTS), was interviewed by the Scottish critic Mary Brennan about the ways NTS moved away from the idea of a building base and has taken theatre *to* Scotland by working with existing venues, within the theatre community, and in site-specific locations, community halls and sports halls, car parks and forests.

In the final new case study for this updated edition of *Programme Notes,* the artist Amanda Coogan interviewed Marina Abramović and the Artistic Director of Manchester International Festival (MIF) Alex Poots about the ways that MIF has opened up new possibilities for artists to think on previously unimaginable scales and work in previously unimaginable spaces, and for audiences to have previously unimaginable experiences.

The collected case studies in *Programme Notes* reflect an exciting range of approaches to the presentation and representation of new forms of theatre and performance. Of course they are by no means the whole picture, and we would be remiss if we did not acknowledge the recent ground-breaking and influential work of other organisations, including National Theatre Wales (whose Artistic Director, John E McGrath, contributed to the first edition of *Programme Notes* in his then role as Director of Contact Theatre), SPILL Festival of Performance, Norfolk and Norwich Festival, and Fuel, along with many others who are brokering relationships with more traditional venues and contexts, and who are, in the process, introducing new audiences to new forms of performance in influential ways.

These new case studies are complemented by an essay by Matt Fenton, Director of Live at LICA (Lancaster Institute for the Contemporary Arts) which reflects on some of the challenges of presenting 'new' theatre in 'old' venues and urges future generations of artists, directors and producers to invent entirely new ways of working.

The edges of creative practice are where the interesting, provocative and contentious experiments can take place. This belief is central to the work of the Live Art Development Agency, and underpins our commitment to reflect and support progressive, marginal and diverse practices. 'Experimental' theatre, in its various forms and manifestations, continues to offer a vibrant site for creative exploration, with, in many instances, massive public and media interest. We hope this volume contributes to awareness and understanding of these issues, instigates debate and conversation, and contributes to the creation of more projects and initiatives which will, in turn, result in future editions of this collection.

Lois Keidan and CJ Mitchell are Co-Directors of the Live Art Development Agency, London

In thinking about the success of the first edition of *Programme Notes*, and how recent its publication seems, I was tempted to ask: *is it not too soon to update it?* However, with the changing nature of Live Art, and the multiple, slippery and hybrid ways in which it works with whatever context is to hand, critiquing and changing that context as it goes, this updating feels timely. The question that seems more pressing is: *who is this powerful book for, and who might it influence, critique and perhaps change?*

The knee-jerk answer is: the directors of major building-based theatres. Those who receive huge annual subsidy are often located in the best-connected city centres surrounded by nightlife and accommodation, and are large, shiny and visible enough to gain real traction with corporate and private giving. As Lois Keidan and CJ Mitchell point out in their introduction, many of these institutions have shifted a great deal in the last decade (well, some of them have); but I suspect it is critical funding policy that affects real change in the short term, alongside organisations' genuine desire to serve the most people in their cities. Our major institutions face multiple and mixed messages: change, explore, experiment, take risks, nurture the new – but also deliver to business plans that are entirely robust, commercially driven and donor-dependent. And lest we forget, these are businesses that employ a lot of people, are to a great extent dependent on box office income, working to city council-set Service Level Agreements, and for whom risk takes on a very different meaning when compared to a venue like my own (outside of town, in an academic context and highly subsidised). I have stated elsewhere that the kinds of risk we have taken at Nuffield Theatre Lancaster (such as opening up our programming budget to artists and local residents; having children curate the gallery; and developing most of our commissioned work outside of the building in close engagement with communities) were possible largely because of the relative stability of the context in which we operate. I suspect the only person's job at risk in these experiments was my own, not an entire organisation's. And buildings can and do close with alarming speed; organisations that take decades to grow and develop can be wound down almost overnight, as recent history reminds us.

Anthony Roberts once memorably asked, in his comparison of the choices facing an audience member in Colchester weighing up the offer between the Mercury Theatre and his own nearby Colchester Arts Centre, *will it be Shakespeare or Franko B?* If you are running the Mercury, and have to fill it six nights a week and twice on Saturdays, how long will your Live Art programming credentials survive? And what, if anything, is a main-house theatre's responsibility to Franko B? Can he, and others like him, access its resources and lovely big stage? Can our major artists who do not work from pre-existing texts, model boxes and known forms really use our best-funded spaces to their own creative ends? Can these institutions accommodate the very different ways of making work, the very different sense of what constitutes the theatrical, of what holds an engagement with audience, even of what constitutes time, in the theatrical space? Can they find a language with which to frame and open up these practices to new audiences (and, much harder, to existing audiences), to validate and promote them? Can there be a context that is not at arm's length (the separately-branded festival of the risky and new, with its microsite and freelance curator, whose success or failure confirms any prejudices one might have about the work and its quality)? Can Live Art and experimental theatre take place at the heart of things – as part of a programme of main-house productions – not just its more palatable elements (the video design, for example) co-opted for mainstream commercial shows? Do we actually want it to?

And to look to ourselves for a moment, why do we, as makers and producers, shy away so readily from known or classic texts? With a few notable exceptions, we have become so suspicious of the grand narratives that we have failed to flip them on their heads to reveal their underbellies, to turn them inside out to see what their insides might reveal. We have failed to use the genre-splicing brilliance of our avant-garde to destroy and then remake these texts, as is our right. Why can we list so few British makers that have taken on the challenge; and why so many German, American, French and Belgian makers who have, often enlisting British performers whose own companies would not consider these texts as viable material?

Many of these issues were hovering behind the discussions at the *Getting It Out There* Conference in Lancaster in May 2012. Like the annual Live Art UK Associates Gathering at BAC (London) that followed it, the event represented a major coming together of British theatre and Live Art makers, programmers, producers and funders. There was a keen sense that things are not easy 'out there', above all for touring work, but that Live Art remains particularly adept at surviving in the cracks and fissures of other disciplines, of finding new ways of getting the radical artist's singular vision in front of an audience. It has been festivals, of all scales (SPILL, Manchester International Festival, LIFT, Wunderbar, Inbetween Time, Fierce) that have seemed more able to accommodate risk, and the formally new, than buildings. Why, really, would any young producer interested in new work, hybrid forms, and meeting audiences in multiple and unexpected ways, want to work solely in a building?

To return to my original question then – *who is this book for?* I do not know if *Programme Notes* will, or even can, influence the directors of major building-based theatres; they are almost certainly too busy. In contrast, the burgeoning public interest in the projects and initiatives outlined in this book, the artists creating this work and the curators, producers and directors supporting them, will all find much of interest here. Ultimately, I hope this book frustrates, enrages and inspires a new generation of artists, directors and producers. Perhaps to take up the leadership of major institutions and venues, but preferably to invent new and better contexts, more equitable and flexible models, more welcoming and egalitarian spaces, rather than seeking to change the existing order from within. That really is playing the long game, and time is precious.

I've always loved working with outsiders. There's something intensely political about closing streets, not for a state visit or a moment of sporting triumph, but for the imagination. It's a provocation and a delight when the public takes to the streets and reminds us all that the city belongs to us.
Helen Marriage, Artichoke, 2007

Programme Notes 2013

The ABC of BAC

**Battersea Arts Centre
over the last ten years**

David Jubb and
David Micklem

We have been invited to add some thoughts to *Programme Notes*, describing some of the ways that Battersea Arts Centre (BAC) develops work and supports artists. We decided to try and spell it out. What follows is not exhaustive. But it is in alphabetical order.

A is for Art

BAC's mission is to invent the future of theatre. We think that theatre can help create community: a community that explores its history and looks to its periphery for inspiration. (See B is for Battersea.) We think it is possible for us all to imagine a better future by putting creativity and invention at the heart of everything we do. We want to make theatre in which our collective imagination is a catalyst to change the world. We think this is possible.

B is for Battersea

A former London borough in SW London with an old Town Hall that has been home to BAC since 1980. Within walking distance of the Town Hall there are £1m houses sitting alongside large housing estates. The building has been a part of civic life since its inception, and over the last 30 years BAC has built strong relationships with many of our neighbours, school teachers, local families, old and young people. We know however that there are many local people who don't know what we do and we are trying to get better at being a place that attracts everyone in the area.

C is for Cook Up Tuck In Take Out

A food metaphor that describes our programme and its three inter-related strands. *Cook Up* is the creative heart of BAC, where work in development, finished shows, food, drink, talks, artists and audiences come together in four seasons a year across the old Town Hall. *Tuck In* defines large-scale shows that are produced or co-produced by BAC, sometimes presented across the entire building: theatrical feasts that take place up to four times a year. *Take Out* is when we exchange the best of our ideas, processes and finished shows with other people and places nationally and internationally.

D is for Debate & for Doing It

The Town Hall was built to house debate, playing host to radical orators such as Charlotte Despard, Emeline Pankhurst and John Burns. BAC keeps a tradition of conversation alive. We like using playful language to describe what we do and to help explore what we might do. We also know that our reputation is built on delivery. We know if we fail to deliver, then playful communication can look like empty rhetoric. Debate is good, but you've also got to Do It.

E is for Experiment

If you can't guarantee the outcome of your work, it's an experiment. If you can, it's a demonstration. We're interested in people trying things out, testing things, taking risks and exploring their creativity in new ways. We like it when these experiments go on to have a longer life outside of Battersea, and when that sense of experiment makes its mark on the wider cultural ecology.

F is for Festival

Ten years ago, BAC's annual programme contained three or four festivals per year largely in three or four spaces. Five years ago, BAC's programme became like a festival most nights of the year across a much greater number of spaces with audiences able to see more than one piece of work in an evening, programming themes and a more flexible use of space. Now when we call something a festival we push the boundaries even further. For example, BAC's *ONE-ON-ONE Festival* contained 10,000 individual performances in the building over two weeks.

G is for Growing

We want to grow things at BAC. New shows, audiences for the work, food for the café. And we want to do this in a resilient way that has an awareness of the environmental impact of our activity. For example, by 2015 we want to grow some of the food we serve in BAC's Café Bar by changing the road that runs alongside the building into a vegetable garden. We want to source the rest from suppliers in London and surrounding counties.

H is for Home & Heritage

BAC regularly draws on its history for inspiration to think about the future. In 1893, there were bedrooms in the attic for the Town Hall Nurse and Assistant Nurse. Now the building provides a home for artists with permanent and temporary bedrooms for up to 24 artists. It also provides a home for creativity, for audiences, staff and artists. We are currently creating an archive that combines our building, civic and cultural history that will be accessible to artists and audiences.

I is for Independence

BAC champions independence and the role of the independent artist and producer. We think that great arts leadership often comes from outside of established arts organisations and we have run programmes such as the Supported Artist programme, The

Homegrown
Photo, James Allen

Uninvited Guests, in association with Lewis Gibson, *Make Better Please*
Produced by Fuel
Photo, Ben Dowden

Independents and Twenty-first-century Leadership to develop independent thinkers.

J is for John Archer
The first black mayor of London, elected in 1913, is one of a long list of radicals who occupied the Town Hall between 1893 and 1965.

K is for Kitchen
To deliver *Cook Up Tuck In Take Out* we are building more kitchens across the building and a garden to grow veg. We see artists, staff and audiences eating together as a central part of our programme and a key role for a theatre rooted in its community.

L is for Leadership
BAC encourages a culture of leadership, supporting individuals in all areas of the organisation to take an active leadership role. We have had double-acts and triple-acts of various kinds leading the organisation. The positives have included greater capacity and richer ideas. The negatives have included lack of clarity and accountability.

M is for Mountford
E.W. Mountford was the Victorian architect responsible for Battersea old Town Hall. We want to preserve and amplify his original design whilst creating facilities for twenty-first-century artists and audiences. Since 2007, BAC Playground Projects have transposed the principles of Scratch (see S is for Scratch) into architecture. These projects are part of a master plan to develop the building in collaboration with architect Steve Tompkins from Haworth Tompkins.

N is for New

It's all been done before. But not by us. And not in the way that we imagine it.

O is for Opera

Jerry Springer the Opera was born at BAC in February 2001 and developed through Scratch (see S is for Scratch). By 2005, it had been seen by 425,000 people in theatres and by 2.4 million people on TV. But we don't do opera anymore really.

P is for Producer

Producers draw together and balance all the different ingredients of making new work. Artists, ideas, participation, audiences, space, marketing, money, funders, politics and administration.

Q is for Queues

We keep ticket prices low with many available for pay what you can (PWYC) to remove barriers to attendance and to ensure queues at box office. We want as many people as possible to experience our work at BAC and as part of our *Take Out* programme or online.

R is for Reinvention

Invention is often about reinventing old ideas in a new context. We recently reinvented our departmental model into a project working structure. Every activity in the organisation is now delivered by project teams made up of staff members with different skills and backgrounds. There are always over twenty projects running at any one time. The reinvented structure gives us more flexibility to adapt and change.

S is for Scratch

BAC created Scratch ten years ago. Scratch is about testing ideas. As well as being a process it is also a way of thinking that embraces experiment and learning. In a theatre context, Scratch means artists sharing work-in-development with an audience; audiences then help enrich the work through their immediate response, through their feedback, sometimes even through getting involved and creating the work themselves. Now adopted and adapted by arts organisations around the world, we are currently developing Scratch Online to open up the process of making theatre to a digital audience.

T is for Teachers

BAC has an Artist-Teacher exchange programme. Some of the most exciting ideas at BAC have emerged out of these collaborations. We advocate for artists and teachers to play a more central role in civic life.

U is for U-turns

When an idea isn't working it's good sometimes to change direction. For example, in 2011 we committed to a producing model that we couldn't afford. We stopped, admitted our mistake and learnt something valuable. We now run a more balanced model comprising touring work alongside BAC-produced and co-produced work.

V is for Victorian Values

In the Lower Hall it says *Non Mihi, Non Tibi, Sed Nobis*. Not For You, Not For Me, But For Us. We like that.

W is for Wallet

BAC encourages everyone who works here to think and act like an entrepreneur and a fundraiser. We are getting smarter at building a portfolio of support.

X is for Xmas Shows
From *World Cup Final 1966* to *Rapunzel* to *Masque of the Red Death* to *1984* to *The Animals & Children Took To The Streets* to *Midnight's Pumpkin,* we pride ourselves on putting on a cracking Christmas show.

Y is for Young People
The future of theatre relies on growing future artists and practice, and it is dependent on there being future audiences. Five years ago, BAC ran a separate participatory strand to its programme. We have now assimilated our participatory strand into our main programme. If we don't produce work that consistently involves and speaks to young people, then we are failing in our mission.

Z is for Zeitgeist
The most commonly used headline by newspaper sub-editors for Battersea Arts Centre is "BAC to the future".

Tinned Fingers
Photo, Neil Baird

Forest Fringe

Andy Field and
Deborah Pearson

Every year there's a moment and the moment goes like this. You are inside in the hall and it's getting quite late and quite dark and we are moving chairs. We are forever moving chairs.

There is the scrape of wooden legs on wooden floor and the sound of performers testing instruments or microphones and projectors don't work and then they do eventually work and lights are swung around and dimmed and raised and tea lights are lit and the doors swing open and shut as people relay messages and ask how much longer it will be and props are lost and then found and those props are hand-drawn illustrations or a baseball bat or seventeen small bottles of Coca Cola or the remains of a trip on the Trans-Siberian railway or lots of glitter or three giant paper boats or a bust card or sometimes there is nothing there is nothing but a man or a woman standing nervously waiting to start to speak but before then more chairs are moved because there are always more chairs to be moved. And outside we've seen the queue of people snaking down the stairs, hundreds of people and we've no idea where they came from but here they are again, improbably and intoxicatingly, here they are again. And as we move we are not artists and production staff, or directors or volunteers or technical managers or assistant technical managers or interns. Here in the half dark, in a hurry, moving chairs, we are a group of people doing everything we can to make sure things are ready in time for all the people outside. And we are tired, we are all tired, and we are underpaid, we are all underpaid, but we don't care. We are just some people having the time of our fucking lives. And that is the moment when you know it is Forest Fringe.

But before that moment arrives there is a little bit of history to cover.

It's 2006 and somewhere in Edinburgh the artist Deborah Pearson is being asked a question by her friends at the Forest Café, a volunteer-run vegetarian café hidden away in the middle of the city. They want to know if she'll run a performance programme during the Edinburgh Fringe in the beautiful, decaying church hall above their café. Their only stipulation is that this won't be part of the official Fringe (a 'fringe of the fringe' as it would later be called by almost everyone apart from us) and that it would be free to everyone; there would be no charge for artists to 'hire' the space, it would be staffed by volunteers, and the shows themselves would be free for audiences. This philosophy is written right through the bone marrow of the Forest Café. It is an absolute must. Deborah says yes and in August of the next year the first Forest Fringe happens.

Now we're skipping forward to 2008 and Deborah is joined by Andy Field, another artist who she met several years earlier in the very average classroom of a university somewhere in Ontario, Canada. He was involved in the first year of Forest Fringe as an artist; he made a piece in a day with a handful of disposable cameras and a borrowed printer and it ended up touring to Brighton and Dublin. Deborah and Andy both knew after that first festival that there was something in this, so they are back to really do something with it. They have got a tiny but important grant from BAC in London and they have used it to rent a flat that they have invited artists to come and stay in whilst they perform. They do not know yet that this festival will be an unexpected and remarkable Edinburgh success, attracting hundreds of people to the old disused church hall and in the process winning a *Herald* Angel. So little is still known about the venue that when the Herald newspaper decide to give it this award, the journalists are not actually sure who it is they are supposed to tell.

It's now 2010 and this rhetorical device is getting a little old. Nonetheless Forest Fringe's momentum has continued to build like Buster Keaton's runaway train. The festival has grown, and Andy and Deborah have grown with it, as have the artists, many of whom have been back every year. By now they all have a better idea of what it is they've made, and why it might be important. Propelled forward on a precarious wave of enthusiasm, they begin to experiment with new Forest Fringe projects beyond the Edinburgh Festival. Towards the beginning of the year they were somewhat improbably listed in *The Stage*'s Top 100 most influential people in theatre, despite Forest Fringe having no staff, no office, and still not being a registered company. When they say Forest Fringe is more a community than an organisation people often don't realise quite how true this is.

Finally we're back here again. It's 2012 and Andy is in an empty office in Bristol and Deborah is in a slightly less empty office in Toronto. We are writing this essay. Pinging drafts back and forth via email like so many other documents over the last five years.

Here and now in 2012 things are changing. We've just finished a residency at the Gate Theatre in London and returned from a major Forest Fringe event in Lisbon. We're talking about going to Austin, Athens and Vancouver. In Edinburgh, despite widespread public support, the Forest Café lost the church space that has always been our Edinburgh home. This year is our first without a performance programme above Forest Café at the Edinburgh Festival. We will still be there, we just won't be There anymore. We still don't have an office of our own, or any staff and if we're completely honest we still aren't sure if we're a registered company.

Forest Fringe continues to slip evasively between most reasonable categorisations of what constitutes an arts organisation. If it really exists anywhere it is in the space between those people that believe in it; the artists, the audiences, even some funders. It is at

Forest Fringe handmade sign
Photo, James Baster

Tania El Khoury, *Fuzzy*
Photo, Ludovic Des Cognets

its heart an unlikely, exhilarating idea. An idea strong enough to drag people from across the country (and sometimes even further) to be a part of it. An idea vivid enough to stand out amidst the eye-stinging neon glare of the Edinburgh Festival. An idea bright enough that it can perhaps even shed some new light on that festival; perhaps even change it. An idea born not from a business plan or a strategy meeting, but from the naivety and necessity of a group of people just getting on and doing it.

Take for example the old church hall in which the idea of Forest Fringe was forged. Wooden floors and high ceilings. Lights hung off the top of the church balcony; eclectic wooden chairs piled haphazardly at the side of the room. Enormous church windows covered in borrowed black fabric or laboriously applied tinfoil.

We came to know this space incredibly well. Through successes and failures we learnt how that space colours the performances that happen in it. Most often those shows that would really glow were those that acknowledged its noisy presence. Shows that didn't try to disguise the space or render it invisible through darkness, but began instead by acknowledging where it was that we were all gathered and why.

The act of gathering together, as much as the stories that were told there, was perhaps the most important thing about Forest Fringe in Edinburgh in those first five years and the most successful shows we had were those that understood that. As such the clumsy architecture of an unconverted church hall and the poor quality of our black out curtains have actually been an absolutely vital part of shaping what Forest Fringe is, what kind of artists it supports and the kinds of radicality that are nurtured there.

From out of the breathless necessity of making something happen we were beginning to discover what was important to us; we were thinking by doing. When the venue began in 2007 we needed to find a way to staff it; not a simple job. Here was a venue which was not officially a Venue, where artists were presenting shows that thanks to a licensing workaround were not even billed officially as Shows. We were completely new and we had no money. By necessity therefore the artists themselves became the most important volunteers we had. Without them the whole thing would have fallen apart.

Consequently in later years, despite the venue having a larger profile, more money, and everything being considerably more official, the artists' personal investment in running the venue has remained crucially important. Nearly all of the artists who work with us volunteer, and through that volunteering they have developed a community. They have sorted recycling and peeled dried paint off plastic chairs. They have pulled staples out of wooden floors and begged disinterested people on the street to take a chance on a free piece of experimental theatre by someone they have never heard of. They continue to be the thing that prevents Forest Fringe from falling apart.

By inviting artists to do more than just present work, what emerged was more than a regular programme of interesting work. It was a shared home and a collective statement about what we value in how we choose to make art. It is a moment when we can come together and try and believe in something important.

And that moment is the moment when everyone is moving chairs. It's the moment when everyone asks if they can help – when nobody knows who exactly they were doing all this for – who exactly it is that they are helping. Forest Fringe is the moment when we are all just helping each other. The opportunity for artists to present work at the Edinburgh Festival for free was a fragile and unlikely one that we are furiously working together to keep alive. And out of that fierce necessity has emerged a profoundly important political imperative. From convenience we

Tim Etchells, *Start a Revolution*
Photo, Hannah Nicklin

learnt a way of doing things that had real meaning within the aggressive commercial marketplace of Edinburgh. A way of doing things that did not expect the exploitation of artists or rehearse the same shallow exchange with audiences. A way of doing that dared hopefully and naively to believe that even systems as large and brutally well established as the Edinburgh Festival can be changed.

And it has changed, in small but significant ways. We won awards that we weren't supposed to be allowed to win. People had to change the rules they'd invented to accommodate us. Critics, keen to cover a place that everyone was talking about, had to experiment with new ways of writing about the work they saw. Large new venues such as Summerhall, Remarkable Arts and Northern Stages were explicit about the influence of Forest Fringe's attitude to presenting work in Edinburgh. Perhaps most fundamentally, a lot of artists who'd sworn off the Edinburgh Festival and Fringe were encouraged to return with a renewed faith in the possibilities that the festival still held, and a greater belief in audiences' appetites for genuinely experimental work.

We began with an opportunity, and some resourcefulness in how to make the most of it. What emerged from that was an idea, one shared amongst a lot of people. And with enough conviction that idea has hopefully started to exert its influence not just on the Edinburgh Festival but on the wider performance culture in this country. That feels exciting to us. And as long as it continues to feel exciting to other people as well, we'll all keep getting on with it, thinking by doing; building new ideas and asking people to believe in them.

I believe it is essential for the healthy development of any society that its culture is not just led by innovations in the market and particularly its control of financially monopolised areas – such as the market control of new technologies – but rather that it continues to refine its vital human communication. This crucial exchange must be radical, unexpected, or previously unknown to truly move us forward. For me, this is the role of experimental theatre.

Robert Pacitti, Artistic Director, Pacitti Company, 2007

Manchester International Festival Presents

Alex Poots, Marina Abramović
and Amanda Coogan
on the Manchester
International Festival

Marina Abramović Presents
(featuring Alastair MacLennan)
Manchester International Festival, 2009
Photo: Joel Chester Fildes

Manchester International Festival launched in 2007 as the world's first artist-led festival of original, new work and special events, commissioning works from across the spectrum of performing arts, visual arts and popular culture.

The Festival has been central to many of the recent developments in the repositioning of interdisciplinary and experimental performance practices in the UK. Instrumental to this is the way it looks at the places and spaces performance can be located, and the siting of uncompromising art in traditional venues such as Manchester Opera House, Whitworth Art Gallery, Manchester Art Gallery and The Lowry.

In both 2009 and 2011 the Festival commissioned Marina Abramović to create major new works: *Marina Abramović Presents* at Whitworth Art Gallery in 2009 and *The Life and Death of Marina Abramović* at The Lowry in 2011. Both works were realized in collaboration with leading performance artists, including Amanda Coogan.

For *Marina Abramović Presents*, Abramović was invited to curate a group show featuring some of the most innovative live artists working today, including Alastair MacLennan, Yingmei Duan, Nikhil Chopra and Terence Koh amongst many others. For the project, the Whitworth emptied every gallery space in order to accommodate the various works. The show began with an hour-long performance initiation with Marina Abramović, leading up to a series of encounters between artists and audience.

The Life and Death of Marina Abramović is a biography of the artist, re-imagined by director Robert Wilson. The show features scenes from Abramović's life and career, from her Serbian childhood to her work as a performance artist, and quotes the practice of the performance artists in the cast. With original and traditional music, including songs written and performed by Antony (Antony and the Johnsons), the show starred Marina Abramović, Willem Dafoe and an international cast of actors and performance artists, including Amanda Coogan, Kira O'Reilly, Elke Luyten, Carlos Soto, Andrew Gilchrist and Ivan Civic.

For *Programme Notes* we invited Amanda Coogan to record conversations with Marina Abramović and MIF's CEO & Artistic Director Alex Poots about the Festival's groundbreaking artistic policy, and some of the implications of this for artists, audiences and the wider cultural landscape of the UK. The following are edited transcripts of conversations held in the dressing rooms of the Carré Theatre in Amsterdam during the European tour of *The Life and Death of Marina Abramović* in 2012.

Marina Abramović, interviewed
by Amanda Coogan

Amanda Coogan: The Manchester International Festival has created totally new possibilities for artists to think on previously unimaginable scales, work in previously unimaginable spaces, and take previously unimaginable risks. What was the commissioning process for *Marina Abramović Presents* or for *The Life and Death of Marina Abramović* and why were you interested in working with the festival on these projects?

Marina Abramović: OK, the first thing is that Alex Poots created the first Manchester International Festival (2007) with *Il Tempo del Postino*. This was pretty revolutionary, and it was really interesting how the different visual artists made something in a theatre setting, and still without compromising their work. And I think *Tempo del Postino* opened the door to so many different things. So the next festival (2009) was actually when Hans Ulrich Obrist and Alex Poots came to me and said, can we do something different and new? We went to Manchester to look at locations and I was proposing to do the seventeen-day *Abramović Presents* with different performance artists and long durational works. And then we went to the Whitworth Gallery, and I said to the Director (Maria Balshaw), OK, I have two solutions, to do just another performance event, or something revolutionary, radical and in a completely different way to everybody else. She said, I would like to do the second choice, which was the really big radical decision, because as you know, there's a huge infrastructure to empty the museum, to put [its collection] in storage and put it back again, but this was the only way that this work can function on that scale. And I think that's what Alex Poots actually creates, a kind of platform for different types of work.

AC: Performance art is a process-based and often radical art form, but with MIF it is being framed in museums and these big theatres. How important is that for you?

MA: To me it is always the same problem that performance art was seen as an alternative form of art, and then being in the museum is a different acceptance and different viewing of that kind of art. So I think that to really be the same as photography, I didn't want to make a kind of street event or work in some alternative space. If the museum showed the art, this is a mainstream art as any other one. So this is why it was important to be in a museum.

AC: Another key characteristic of MIF is their commitment to interdisciplinarity, to different disciplines coming together. How did that work with *The Life and Death of Marina Abramović*?

MA: You know, it's interesting that Alex Poots already wanted to do *Life and Death*, but said 'you [first] have to be introduced to the public in a certain way.' So it was a long-term kind of concept, from even before *Abramović Presents*. Then *Abramović Presents* had a lot of success and this created a platform and other theatre producers became interested to actually sponsor *The Life and Death* and to make it happen.

AC: But what is your thinking on this interdisciplinarity, the relationships between performance art from the visual arts and from theatre?

MA: I think this is a long story. We always forget that the theatre of Tadeusz Kantor, La MaMa, The Wooster Group, the really old-fashioned historical theatres, they have so many performative elements there already and there are many times [when] performance artists actually participated in their works. Joan Jonas worked with The Wooster Group for such a long time. When Jan Fabre started his career his inspiration was performance, and Pina Bausch and Anne Teresa De Keersmaeker included enormous amounts of performative elements. So that is like a kind of history of how things get into each other. Right now it's interesting that there is a reverse, we actually have pure performance artists playing pure theatre, so we actually accept the artificiality of theatre as another reality. And this never happened before. In my own other biography [projects] I was doing so much performance inside [the plays], there was always so much real performance. But now, theatre becomes something very fascinating to me because it is very much to do with metaphors, with the sets of images, to create some sort of almost mystic elements inside. I mean it really works.

AC: Do you think this has influenced your practice?

MA: I don't know if it influences practice, that's another question, but it is very interesting, because we are still performing this piece. But I have to say I learned so much from Robert Wilson and I never could have the patience just to sit and wait for the bloody lights or these sets, because performance is all about having [the] public and then everything happens. I would never rehearse, but here the rehearsals and how the images build and how the public react and how they get this information... it's quite interesting to see what we can do with this in our own practice.

AC: What is the relationship with the audience in *The Life and Death* and how is this different to your 'normal' practice?

MA: It is interesting that Bob put in so many elements which actually have nothing to do with my life, or my death, and created some kind of transcendental key so that anybody can project his biography onto this biography. I mean the lobster, I asked what is the meaning of the lobster, it's not in my life, but then to actually discover that the lobster is actually very much to do with Jack Smith which is influencing Bob Wilson's life, so

Marina Abramović Presents
Manchester International Festival, 2009
Photo, Joel Chester Fildes

he put that in. Also, somebody was saying to me, 'the biography really moves me, I don't talk to my brother or my mother, and they also die finally', so you take something that is very personal but you really create a new version of the image, and at the end it's not anymore about me it's about everything else.

AC: Your relationship to the audience was much more direct in *Abramović Presents* than in *The Life and Death*.

MA: But you know it's so funny that so many people say, 'oh my god, you're completely diminished from the piece... everything emotional is removed, you're like automatic there', you know, all this. But I always wanted to be a tool in some sense, to give up this control. Every time when I'm there I'm trying really to be present one hundred percent and I feel the audience, but there is really to me the two unique moments that I feel that are more close to me than anything else, and this is the bed scene (A4 – The Story about the hospital) and when we are in the sky levitating (Epilogue: Funeral) when the audience is literally open-eyed and open-mouthed. That moment is incredible because you understand that the audience really are somewhere else, we transport them in another space from reality, and that moment before the curtain goes [down] is just incredible. And I'm living every evening for that moment.

AC: Does the Manchester International Festival offer a very specific structure for new work?

MA: You know the one condition the Manchester Festival has is to be always new and presented for the first time in Manchester, nowhere else. And this is what is so unique, so when you want to see something that nobody has seen before, you go to Manchester Festival. And then from *Abramović Presents* developed a completely other body of work, which is *Abramović Method* which I just had now in Milan. To understand long durational work the public have to perform it themselves, to understand where the mind is going and what is happening. It's four groups of twenty-one people, who are the normal public who come to the museum, they have to dress in lab coats in the *Abramović Method* and they have to give all their watches and everything away and then they have to do little exercises and after that they have to perform sitting, standing and lying. And they have no way to escape except in themselves, they have to stay there two and a half hours. In two and a half months, eight thousand people did this. So now I want to create this *Abramović Method* everywhere in the world, because I don't need to be there anymore, so one public is performing and another public is watching, to mobilise the system. This came directly from *Abramović Presents*.

AC: What do ideas of innovation and risk mean in relation to MIF and *Abramović Presents* and *The Life and Death*?

MA: You know it's incredibly important to invent something and to go to unknown territory, and to take the risk to do it in front of the public. It's directly related to failure, because if you don't risk you don't fail, and it's very easy to do things that you know are good. But at the same time this leads to repetition. But if you actually invent something that is new then you have to be ready to fail. Right here in this same theatre twenty-nine years ago I made the biggest bullshit in my life with Ulay, for the same Hollande Festival, with this piece called *Positive Zero,* and it was such a terrible thing. I was so proud of this piece but after the first fifteen minutes I started realising how shit it was, the whole thing, and I could not stop because we had to play three nights. I was sick every single night and I fought a temperature, I was sick for months, but that piece was really important because it led to a completely new body of work, but we had to do that.

AC: Did this lead to *Nightsea Crossing*?

MA: Yes. And it's very interesting, and really we fail grandiose, completely. But really that idea of the failure it's kind of very important. This is how I understood why it is so important [to work with] long duration, because we need, as a performer, as the public needs, time to get into that kind of zone, but that's something that you can't speed up. In my case *The Artist is Present* is exactly the same, the first month everybody was busy and nobody was [paying attention, they were] just passing by, the second month we are getting paid attention, and then third month, third month kicks off. And that's the thing, it's unique, there's no way out. Another thing that Manchester offers is a unique combination of people that normally would actually not even know each other and communicate, because they are really looking for people who are not even friends, but would be an interesting combination to see what kind of new work comes through. And that's very important. That's what Alex was doing, like he would combine the musician together with the filmmaker, filmmaker together with the director and that's amazing.

AC: It's a very special kind of ability to pick those things that will be successful or artists who will be able to work together.

MA: And that's why I think he is quite amazing, Alex Poots, he had this vision and he had this enormous passion for what he's doing, that really makes a huge difference.

Amanda Coogan: I talked with Marina about the
ways Manchester International Festival has opened up new
possibilities for artists to think in previously unimaginable
scales, to work in previously unimagined spaces, and with
previously unimaginable risks. What was your thinking at
the conception of MIF about these kinds of interdisciplinary
practices and experimental processes, and how has it developed
over the last three festivals?

Alex Poots: The bit I am most careful about at the outset is
which artists to invite, who is imaginative, talented and still
creating work at their peak. I would ask, 'what's your unrealised
project, the thing you've always wanted to do, the thing that
everyone said was not possible? We could try and do that'. So,
when Marina said that she wanted Bob Wilson to direct her
death, and when Bob said, only if we direct her life, I said, yes, I'll
definitely do that. At that point what I really cared about was
making sure the musical aspect of this project would be as robust
as Marina's artistic practice and Bob's directing. I wanted one
auteur, one musical voice to preside over it, and that was Antony
[Hegarty]. So then you've got this triumvirate of creatives.

AC: And that seems key to the kinds of projects MIF does –
there is this magnificent collision of strong practitioners that
maybe have never worked together before, who come together to
make these very unique projects.

AP: But they always come together, not because it's good for
marketing (a mistake that some people can make in analysing

it), or for the sake of 'collaborating' (not an end in itself), but because 'it's a necessity'. Marina needed Bob, and actually to do something really unlike anything he's done in the last ten to fifteen years, Bob needed Marina, because she's the catalyst to him, and he's the creator and frame of the vision. They both said it needed music, and they've both been doing their own respective work at the highest level for forty years, so I wanted the project to not only have a remarkable composer, but to also be cross-generational, all of which led to Antony.

Another example is the company Punchdrunk who create immersive theatre. I remember being completely wowed by Punchdrunk's work, and when I met Adam Curtis, the TV documentary filmmaker, I said wouldn't it be amazing if, rather than what normally happens in immersive theatre, where as the individual audience member you make up your own art as you wander through it, there was a story that you followed in an immersive way. Adam was very interested in telling stories that weren't just on TV in a two-dimensional way – he wanted people to be enveloped in them. Because Adam couldn't do it without Felix Barrett (of Punchdrunk), and Felix couldn't do it without Adam, the collaboration [*It Felt Like A Kiss*, 2009] was a very specific way to achieve the artistic outcome they wanted – a result neither could achieve without the other.

AC: In forming MIF, or MIF coming into being, was this your agenda, was this your vision? That you would be taking different practices and making a soup?

AP: No, it was always an artist-led festival wanting to produce ambitious new work. I think the artist's desire to explore their practice and to evolve their practice can often lead them into areas where they need other people to help them realise it. And that's where MIF comes in. But we have had productions that

Marina Abramović Presents (featuring Jamie Isenstein and Ivan Civic, respectively)
Manchester International Festival, 2009
Photos, Joel Chester Fildes

are very singular in their vision. When Victoria Wood wrote and directed her new production, *That Day We Sang*, she wanted to achieve this single-handedly and it was a very successful show, and one that we fully supported. Snoop Dogg did it all himself, with *Doggystyle*. I always try to start with a leading artist who's at the top of their game, and who has the imagination to really take their art form onto another level or further down the road.

AC: A different direction.

AP: Yes, or further down the same direction.

AC: And how important is the framing for you in terms of taking experimental practices and putting them in museums or big theatres? I am thinking of *Il Postino* and how visual artists were put into a different framing, or *Marina Abramović Presents*, where you're taking process-based performance from the visual arts that often happen in alternative spaces and giving it the framing of the museum. And then of course this piece, *The Life and Death of Marina Abramović*, at The Lowry.

AP: The Whitworth exhibition of 2009 and *The Life and Death* is an interesting story. Marina and Bob asked, through Marina, if *The Life and Death* was something we'd be interested in at MIF. One of the earliest things I said to her was that a lot of people in the UK know about Bob's practice in opera, music and theatre, but the area that you and the people around you represent is much more underground, much more edgy, and I didn't want this to go unnoticed in the production. So I suggested to Marina that we introduce audiences to this long durational performative work that most people don't know anything about. That's what led to *Marina Abramović Presents* in 2009, one of the most important exhibitions we've done. It was to give people time to learn about this important area that has often been slightly off the radar.

AC: Marina talked about that as well, how she put it was that you felt it needed to be introduced.

AP: Yes, it was like a story that we needed... and I wanted it to have the gravity that theatre has. We've got the West End and offshoots, and the National Theatre, but we've not got a national performance art centre, and I wanted the two worlds to have parity.

AC: So what kind of challenges do these things, this mixture, bring to the audience and to the artists as well?

AP: Well, one challenge is, what is it and how do you describe it? Because once the piece is conceived, you want to interest an audience. Yet before it's been made you don't really know quite what it's going to be – is it going to more in this artistic area or another, and however you describe it before it's made will probably be wrong. So you have to find a momentum to the attraction of the show that almost snowballs through the bewilderment of: is it a gallery show? Is it a musical? Or is it an opera? But Willem Dafoe is in it, so is it a piece of theatre? But what can make it is its audacity and the confidence of what it's trying to be and do and who's in it – all its different elements. The kind of level of talent in this show is rare, which is actually why it's such a difficult show to tour because each cast member is top dog in their respective worlds.

AC: As solo artists we're so used to being the boss of our own show and to step into this we have to remember that actually we're a cast member. But it's such an interesting project to be involved in.

AP: You know, on this production I feel like it's in the right area to potentially be a show that could be remembered in several years time. If in your lifetime, as a presenter, you have three or four of those, you're fortunate. And if it doesn't prove to be one, I know everyone gave it their all.

AC: What kind of responsibility do you think that 'mainstream producers' have towards investing in experimental artists or experimental processes, in terms of the vision that MIF is putting out there?

AP: Well you see I don't invest in areas of experimentation; I always invest in an artist, or group of. What led me to you and your amazing practice were Marina and Bob saying, would you go on this journey with us to make this show. To me the logical story of getting to opening night had to involve you from the start, so your practice could be seen and understood before incorporating it into this other thing. And then suddenly I thought OK, great, there's the potential here for a great exhibition in 2009 and a great show in 2011, and there's a whole journey going on that has a kind of curious logic to it rather than a literal didactic logic.

AC: So you're talking about looking at this from a radically different perspective, from the engagement with the artist and the artist's practice?

AP: Yes, for me it's all about the artist, it's not about me or my vision, or some theme or framing device. What I'm interested in is that next summer, MIF presents 18 to 20 great artists (or groups of), making great work. You know if you trust the artist, for a thing that is as risky as a festival of entirely new work, you need to give yourself as much chance of succeeding as you can, and the best way I've found to achieve this is to trust really good artists because they're the best chance you have of presenting good things. If you don't let their natural instincts and intuitions flow through, and if you start putting up brick walls because you're trying to impose a theme or some conceit you harbour, then you risk denaturing the artistic, creative process.

AC: MIF put in some pretty spectacular structures to make those visions happen though as well.

AP: That's why we only do 18 to 20 projects every two years. Many festivals will have 100 or more, but my mantra is less is more. Do a few things the best you possibly can.

AC: Ms Abramović accuses you of being a visionary.

AP: No. The skill I need to try and keep developing is identifying really good artists and finding the best ways to support them, that's a big part of my job. I look to see who I think is great, ask them to come in, and then look after them when they're in my house.

Theatre Without Walls

Mary Brennan in conversation with Vicky Featherstone of National Theatre of Scotland

In 2004, Vicky Featherstone became the first ever Artistic Director of the newly-launched National Theatre of Scotland (NTS). Unlike similarly-tagged ventures elsewhere, NTS had no bricks-and-mortar theatre to call its own. And to begin with, Featherstone didn't even have a proper, permanent office.

She laughs, remembering how she walked into an empty room in Glasgow's city centre with a mobile phone in one hand, and a Muji notebook in the other. "No furniture, not even a chair. So I just sat on the floor, thinking 'it's my job to start a national theatre...' And that could have been a terrifying 'zero moment'. But really, all I could see were possibilities. We were going to make a national theatre of, and for, Scotland from scratch – how exciting was that? And even now, when I'm moving on, I still feel excited by what we've started. And by what I've learned about the value of theatre, and the making of theatre, along that way."

As of 2013, Featherstone will relocate south where she will be the next Artistic Director at the Royal Court Theatre in London. If this lends a kind of poignancy to this conversation (in mid-December 2012), it also allows Featherstone a chance to pinpoint aspects of her time at NTS that especially surprised or challenged her.

If the new venture came without walls, a roof or a fixed proscenium arch, it did come with stacks of baggage. "The hunger to have a National Theatre of Scotland had been growing and intensifying for ages," she says. "But wanting isn't the same as having. Scotland has a very complex and diverse infrastructure in terms of theatre – buildings and provision. Some towns had purpose-built venues, others depended on town halls or community centres having stages and technical facilities. Some venues had resident companies, some hosted touring productions, but there were parts of the country that never saw any live theatre at all. If we were to connect with people all across Scotland, truly be a national theatre for them, then we had to engage with that diversity, that unpredictability. For me, the genius of the NTS model – which came, really, from the theatre community itself – was the determination not to have a building. There were to be no barriers, no boundaries. Nothing that would shackle the enterprise to one place and one place only. Accept that and immediately you are forced to think about the kind of work you need to make, if you intend to have theatre actively inhabit the country of Scotland."

Home, the first ever NTS production (staged in February 2006) was a ground-breaking statement of that intent. There had been all kinds of speculation as to the where, when and what of Featherstone's inaugural showing. Pressure too, which – now that she is no longer in post – can be revealed as sadly tinged with a resentful hostility in some quarters: indeed, the fact that the English Featherstone had the gift of shaping and establishing such a talismanic addition to the Scottish cultural profile would continue to invite antagonism and reproach from certain veteran commentators throughout her tenure. "I always felt it was from a small group of people," she says, "and didn't actually represent the relationships that we had created around Scotland. But it brought positive aspects as well: it has left me thinking more, and differently, about issues of national identity, and very aware of how we, as theatre-makers, can – or should – express these, and other social issues."

The heart of such matters, she reckons, lies in the stories you tell. And *Home* exemplifies this in ways that are still talked about – and imitated – in communities all across Scotland. Instead of one red-carpeted premiere in a selected venue, there were ten different productions located in a scatter of sites that stretched from a disused glass factory in Caithness to a scary wood in East Lothian by way of a ferry – with fiddlers on board – from Lerwick harbour and an old, 1950s ballroom in Dundee. It's probably fair to say that Featherstone looks back on *Home* with a mix of glee, relief and amazement. Nothing like it had ever been attempted before. Moreover the legacy of that one dank and chilly February night is likely to be felt for decades to come, given the intensity and breadth of community involvement that was wrought into the process at every level.

"In my mind," she says, "each of these productions was like a beacon. One of those fires that used to be lit up, in a chain, across the countryside – a kind of message that could be seen for miles and miles. And part of that message was about cutting through all the stultifying speculation about our first production. Whatever else, we were determined not to be defined, theatrically or otherwise, by one single production on only one night in one specific place, and to one particular audience. This was about ownership. When you decide that no one can ever 'own' the whole NTS experience – and no one was ever going to be able to see all ten parts of *Home* – then you give over ownership to everyone, as it were. *Home* was just the beginning. The entire country was going to be our 'venue'. Everybody across Scotland was to have the chance to connect with NTS at some point or on some level. Going along to see a touring show in their area was the obvious connection. But maybe taking part in a skills workshop would forge that link, or even someone just listening to a grandchild who was part of a community outreach project would be enough to build awareness. This was about reaching out, persuading people that a national theatre wasn't just FOR them but it could also be ABOUT them. I know, I know – it sounds simplistic, almost naive. But we all felt that the vision we had of 'national' had to go beyond that complacent 'well-made theatre staging well-made plays for [and she laughs mischievously here] a well-made audience.' There was a huge responsibility to break out of that mould, a huge ambition to find the best ways, the new ways, of bringing audiences into theatre. Even if they were standing in a car park, and not sitting on some plush seat in a nineteenth-century palace to the art."

The brief she gave to the ten Scottish directors she recruited for *Home* was both open-ended and precise: they would have total artistic freedom in terms of how each production interpreted 'home' as a theme – but there had to be a genuine and involved relationship with the community that each director and NTS team were assigned to. "So often," she says, "you feel that a piece has just been parachuted in. That couldn't be allowed to happen with *Home*. Each piece had to have a relevance, thematically and artistically, to the place and the community it was in. It sounds so simple, so straightforward – and obvious! – when you say it. But the challenges are always tricky, and tough. There's no easy template either. You have to go in and listen. Hear the stories that people tell you, and then find a process that makes those stories into a piece of theatre. You just have to keep questioning your actions and ideas. 'What do you want an audience to feel? How are you going to move them from one idea to the next? How do you take responsibility for that, so as not to leave them challenged in a counter-productive way?' You take it back to the fundamentals. Then you can invent and

Black Watch, Cameron Barnes facing front
Photo, Manuel Harlan

Black Watch, Scott Fletcher facing front
Photo, Manuel Harlan

invent – before working out which ideas are worth sticking with, because of how they get to the meat of those stories."

She continues. "*Home* didn't just bring the directors' stories, it also brought them into close contact with context. We all sort of knew that Scotland had a wonderful tradition of popular theatre and entertainment – much-loved, highly distinctive pantomime, variety shows, ceilidhs actually, as well as a sense of identity in the widespread music-making and storytelling. I think we learned to take all that on board, not just in some aspects of *Home*, but in subsequent productions – *Black Watch*, for one, *The Strange Undoing of Prudencia Hart* (which drew on the rollicking energies of traditional folk-ballads) is another. At the same time, we hadn't turned our back on proscenium-arch theatres or classic texts. Because we weren't just listening to the stories and communities – we were listening to the artists, to the companies, to the venues, that were already part of theatre in Scotland. It was never our idea to do what they were already doing. Our role was to release potential, if you like. Provide support – sometimes financial, sometimes in the form of technical resources or expertise – so that artists, companies, could push beyond what they had already achieved. I remember Dominic Hill, when he was still at Dundee Rep, talking to me about Ibsen's *Peer Gynt* and these wonderful, rip-roaring ideas he had about how you could do it – then saying that it was really far too big an undertaking for the Rep to do. But an NTS co-production...! When something like *Peer Gynt* comes to fruition, proves to be a success with critics and audiences in Scotland and beyond, that makes for some of our most joyous work, I think."

'Listening' is one of the words that peppers Featherstone's buoyantly affectionate look back over eight years at the helm of NTS. The proof of how effectively she listened – and heard what was really being said, especially by the young or

inexperienced talents who approached her – can be found
in the range of talents who jumped at the chance to be a
part of the operation and the range of work that NTS has
staged all across Scotland from 2006. There have been
Edinburgh International Festival premieres, visionary co-
productions with disabled artists, large-scale family friendly
shows that encouraged children's theatre companies to flex
their creative muscles, hire more than two actors and revel
in the joys of high-end stage sets, animations, music and
dynamic marketing... and, of course, there have been the site-
specific adventures that morphed unlikely spaces into magic
portals, so that an airport or a car park, a high-rise tower block
or a forest, became not just a theatre, but the National Theatre
of Scotland.

"You can have all kinds of conversations about community
involvement," says Featherstone. "Or about 'immersive'
theatre. But in the end it has to be about making art. Making
the best art possible, otherwise it all collapses. Loses integrity.
Feels phoney. When we did *Enquirer* [a verbatim collage of
interview material that reflected the noble aspirations and
disreputable practices of the newspaper industry], people came
into this office on the top floor of a building that overlooked
the River Clyde and went 'this venue is just incredible!' And
it was. But when we moved the play to London, it went into
a really dingy office space, and it had just as much impact.
And if anything, it worked even better when it went out on
radio, because there was nothing between the listener and
the words. *Enquirer* was a success because I had an amazing
team working with me to make the stories we had into the
best possible theatre. Like with *Black Watch*, which has toured
and toured globally, but which audiences – venues – still
want. I suppose the process of making *Black Watch* became
something of a 'signature process' for us as Scotland's national
theatre. These were Scotland's own stories, real stories from

Jump
Photo, Tim Morozzo

Home Shetland, directed by Wils Wilson
Photo, Pete Dibdin

Ménage a Trois, Claire Cunningham and Gail Sneddon
Photo, Kenny Mathieson

men who'd been in this legendary Scottish regiment, and we found a way to tell them as theatre. We proved that the personal is not parochial, it's universal – but you can't be fearful with it. I think you have to go after the kind of energy you had as a child, when you let your imagination run free and you played games of wonderful make-believe. I think, I hope, that's the kind of permission NTS has given to artists and to audiences: to take risks and be empowered by them. I remember, watching that first production of *Black Watch* in that Drill Hall in Edinburgh – and watching the audience, their reactions – and heaving a huge sigh of relief. Because I had this vision of what I'd always wanted theatre to do, and here it was, doing it. I saw men moved to tears, I spoke with soldiers' wives and girlfriends who told me they now understood all kinds of things that their menfolk had never spoken about – and the collective force of what we had all shared... the effect of that is so hard to put into words, but it felt transformative, and liberating. That experience, actually my entire experience at NTS, has changed the way I feel about theatre. Scotland is a thoroughly demotic country. It despises elitism, and it fights for a democracy within the arts and for audiences. There's no snobbery against the popular forms – or against the radical ones either. That climate made a 'theatre without walls' not only possible, but essential I think. Helping that into being as the National Theatre of Scotland – and apparently over two thirds of the population now know what NTS is – has been a revelation to me. I'm still in love with this job, and with Scotland – but there are brilliant people in place who will make sure things move on without me. And I'll be taking what I've learned from my time here to the Royal Court – and who knows, we might be performing in the local car park yet!"

Ursula Martinez, *Show Off*
Photo, Hugo Glendinning

Programme Notes 2007

Introduction

Lois Keidan, Daniel Brine
and David Micklem
(from Programme Notes, 2007)

Programme Notes is about furthering dialogues and collaborations between the theatrical mainstream and artists from the independent sector.

Over the last decade or so there has been a growing sense that theatre venues across the UK are expressing greater interest in work that pushes at the edges of our expectations of what theatre could be. Some venues are actively programming more experimental works. Others are expressing a keenness to explore the opportunities for taking their audiences on new journeys. Whilst it is acknowledged that this work is challenging, sometimes difficult, often compelling, always engaging, it is also work that can attract new audiences, offer new experiences, and add bold new strands to a venue's programme. Whether it is the National Theatre collaborating with Shunt, Duckie's events at the Barbican, Noble & Silver at Soho Theatre, or Gob Squad working on the main stage of Nottingham Playhouse it is increasingly evident that theatres in the UK are excited about a new set of relationships with experimental artists and companies.

And more and more experimental companies themselves are interested in changing and innovating in different contexts. No longer content to occupy only studio theatres, site specific locations, or 'the fringes' of our culture, many of today's artists are equally excited by the possibilities of working in main houses and on centre stages, re-imagining the kinds of roles they can play, the kinds of audiences they can talk to, and the kinds of stories they can tell them.

There has perhaps never been a better time to progress the place and profile of independent theatre-makers in the UK, or for our theatre venues to take a fresh look at what they can do, and how they can do it.

So, how can more theatre venues and experimental companies respond to such shifts in the theatrical landscape of the UK and invest in our cultural future? How can theatres that are intrigued by the possibilities of new theatrical forms and new relationships with audiences be encouraged to not only take more risks but be better equipped to do so? And how can those theatres more resistant to new ways of working be encouraged to try something different?

Programme Notes has been created as a resource to contribute to these debates and stimulate interest by reflecting models of exciting and innovative relationships at work in different places in the UK.

In a series of commissioned case studies and essays, influential artists, producers, and commentators have been invited to consider the nature, breadth and value of contemporary theatre practices, and to write about specific projects from their own experiences and perspectives, providing practical insights into programming initiatives and audience development work that have connected the mainstream with experimental theatre.

In their introductory essays for *Programme Notes*, theatre critic Lyn Gardner writes about the tidal wave of new theatre practices and their exciting relationships with audiences in the UK, suggesting that 'perhaps not since the late 1960s has Britain's theatre culture been quite so fluid, quite so open to the possibilities of the new'; whilst the writer and director Tim Etchells talks about the potential of contemporary theatre to connect with its audiences in previously unimagined ways: its capacity 'to pick people up and really take them places'. The case studies and interviews provide a fascinating understanding of different approaches to developing new ways of working within more established venues, arts centres and festivals in the UK.

Programme Notes is concerned with what a truly forward-looking theatre might be; in the artistic aspirations, new approaches and cultural complexity of its practitioners; in the critical and media contexts for new work; in the nature of contemporary audiences and the opportunity to develop them through new work.

Programme Notes is a handbook for artists and commentators, and indeed anyone interested in the nature of theatre in the UK today. But it is especially a resource for theatre programmers, artistic directors and venue managers, with the aim of sharing knowledge and stimulating thinking around a broader range of new and emergent theatrical practices.

Lois Keidan and Daniel Brine, Live Art Development Agency
David Micklem, Arts Council England

There is something stirring

Lyn Gardner

There is something stirring. A huge mechanical elephant comes to London and up to a million people come out onto the streets to play and laugh and wonder, the numbers swelled not by reviews in the broadsheet papers, but by word of mouth and hundreds of thousands of images sent by the camera phone – that modern, technological Pied Piper.

At the Barbican, Bobby Baker sells out the main auditorium and is invited back again. Forced Entertainment – ignored for years by the mainstream – suddenly attracts glowing reviews and is discovered and feted by a whole new generation of theatre-goers, many of whom weren't even born when the company was founded. The Fierce Festival in Birmingham and the National Review of Live Art in Glasgow offer audiences – hungry for a theatre experience which doesn't just pin them like butterflies on a plush red velvet seat – a taste of something very different. The British Council champion and send abroad as cultural ambassadors a raft of companies and live artists who most first-string theatre critics in this country won't even have heard of, let alone seen.

Yes, there is undoubtedly a shift going on. Perhaps not since the late 1960s has Britain's theatre culture been quite so fluid, quite so open to the possibilities of the new and more willing to break the rules set by a theatre establishment that still clings to late nineteenth- and early twentieth-century notions of theatre practice, like a bedraggled shipwreck survivor clinging to a rotting plank of wood. We have lived too long in a theatre culture in which the past is valued over the future, the classic over the contemporary, and where the point of reference is John Osborne, David Hare and Tom Stoppard rather than Impact, Welfare State International and Pip Simmons. This is a world where Stanislavsky has been celebrated and Artaud ignored.

But there are signs that the dominance is being broken. If the mid 1990s were seen as golden age in playwriting with the emergence of new voices such as Sarah Kane and Mark Ravenhill, the early part of the twenty-first century has been a similarly revolutionary time in theatre's search for form and a new relationship between performer and audience. The outside has suddenly become the inside, and the fringe is infiltrating the mainstream on a scale not previously seen or even imagined.

Companies such as Shunt and Punchdrunk have been taken by the National Theatre, puppetry embraced by the RSC, burlesque by the Barbican. In London, the Chelsea Theatre reinvents itself as a live art venue and Home has people knocking on its door eager to engage with the intimacies of performance in a room in a family house rather than a theatre. In Sheffield, shows such as *Shadowmouth* – a collaboration between writer Meredith Oakes and director/choreographer Dominic Leclerc – are part of a growing and increasingly important strand of work in which neither the word nor the physical has the upper hand. The theatre of transgression has entered the mainstream via the craze for burlesque, and the work of Duckie and individual artists such as Ursula Martinez are taking live art practice to audiences who may not know what the term 'live art' means but who certainly like what they see. In the capital, young companies are deserting traditional pub theatres for found spaces (derelict warehouses and factories, church crypts) and on the Edinburgh fringe – that most commercial of market places – the most successful new venue of recent years has been Aurora Nova @ St Stephens, where European companies such as Derevo and Fabrik have found not just a home but a devoted audience.

What we are seeing is a movement which has the potential to put theatre and live art right at the centre of our culture as it breaks down all the old divisions and suspicions between theatre and live art, the playhouse and the gallery, the text and the visual and physical. One of the joys of a piece such as Marisa Carnesky's *Ghost Train* – played out on a purpose-built fairground ride – is the fact that it cannot be classified because it breaks all the rules and defies all expectation. It is its very 'differentness' which distinguishes it, as much as its sexual politics and its games with high and low art. It is its 'differentness' that also lends it an accessibility and diversity. Unlike traditional theatre which takes place behind the closed doors of the playhouse, it shuts nobody out, and it allows the audience to take themselves to the event. It has a plasticity which ensures that it is what every individual member of the audience thinks it is. Similarly the *Sultan's Elephant* could be read in many ways, not least as an artistic occupation of the streets, an invasion that disrupts the spectacle of everyday life and reclaims the streets of the city as a place that belongs to us and where we can play and dream. This is art which allows us ownership of our own lives and own imaginative processes.

The thing that makes this surge of interest in 'differentness' and experiment particularly encouraging is that it appears to be driven by audiences rather than by critics, commentators or even venues. We all lag far behind. We live in a world which is becoming increasingly homogenous, where one high street in one town looks very much like a high street in one several hundred miles away and a cup of coffee bought in Newcastle tastes just like one bought in Truro. It is a place where one Hollywood blockbuster has the same special effects and looks pretty much like another Hollywood blockbuster. Novels and plays are often sold on the premise that if you like this, you will also like that because after all one piece of chick lit is pretty much like another and if you liked *Art* you will certainly like *Heroes*.

Yet increasingly it seems to me that audiences see through these marketing scams and hunger for cultural experiences which not only are different but which have an authenticity. They crave the intimacy and emotional connectedness that live art can deliver, but which is mostly absent from the traditional well-made play produced in a Victorian playhouse where from the back row of the stalls everyone on stage looks Lilliputian. How can such an experience compete with the intimacy of Kira O'Reilly's encounters at the National Review of Live Art in which she invited audience members to either cut her or hold her? The audience is no longer merely a passive spectator, they are part of the event itself. They make it, alongside the artist, and every performance is unique because the participants are always different. And it is not just one to one performances that work on this premise – a piece such as Robert Pacitti's *A Forest*, doesn't just perform to its audience, it implicates us by bringing us into the circle and making us voice our innermost secrets and longings.

It is clear that such encounters are addictive. The scripted play seems tame once the audience has tasted this power and the possibility of interaction. We are no longer content to sit quietly in our seats when we can storm the stages. Once we have learned this new theatrical vocabulary, we want more opportunities to hear it and speak it, we no longer find it satisfying merely to stick to other people's scripts. What's more, there are many more people who are comfortable with this new theatrical language. The rise of the Theatre Studies A Level that gives as much weight to the work of the David Glass

Ensemble and Forced Entertainment as it does to the well-made play is creating a new generation of theatregoers and theatre-makers who are at home with experimentation, the devised, the physical and the visual and who instinctively understand the connections between a theatre tradition and a gallery tradition. Many of these young people are going on to degree courses in advanced theatre practice and creating a substantial wave of new practitioners who don't want to make drama but who do want to make theatre, who couldn't care less about plays but who care very passionately about live art.

This is potentially a brave new world in which we live, made all the more exciting by the rise of a new generation of creative producers who eschew traditional theatre and are forging new partnerships and ways of working that encompass live art and work in non-theatre spaces. It is a welcome sign that even Nicolas Hytner, artistic director of that bastion of the theatre establishment, the National Theatre, is far less afraid than his predecessors of the new, the experimental and transgressive and has been spotted checking out Duckie as well as the latest play at the Royal Court.

Even so, I am afraid. Audiences and these new producers are often far braver than the programmers, funders and critics, and we have also been here before: after all this is not the first time that an alternative theatre and live art culture has flourished. The late Sixties and Seventies saw a flowering of companies and individual artists who eschewed traditional theatre for more experimental modes, and even in the 1980s – supported largely by the ICA and a radical arts centre tradition – companies were still being founded to explore new theatrical languages. With the glorious exception of Forced Entertainment, regarded by many in Europe and the US as *the* great British theatre company of the last 30 years, there have been few survivors. Perhaps it was not surprising, after all that was an era when those who ran our theatres and most critics came from a Leavis tradition which values the literary and the literal over the language of dreams and ritual and the personal story and experience. As David Glass has observed, the history of theatre is written by the victors, and the victors have always been the text-based play, the writer and the director who realises the writer's vision. Some of the innovations have been integrated – at least superficially – into the mainstream, but most of it has disappeared and along with it the traditions and teachers who could hand down the expertise. It means that each new generation of theatrical experimenters has had to reinvent the wheel all over again.

The difference this time is the sheer scale of what is happening. When up to a million people spontaneously take to the streets to watch the *Sultan's Elephant*, or you see people besieging the box office at Aurora Nova hoping to get a ticket to see Derevo and Duckie sells out at the Barbican, you know that this time change is really possible, and that we can create a bolder, broader and more invigorating and inclusive culture in which theatre and live art have a central place. The audiences are already storming the barricades, it is up to the rest of us to give them a helping hand because the revolution has already started without us, and it would be such a pity to miss it.

GRAN

Empty Stages: Venice
Photo: Hugo Glendinning and Tim Etchells

Some people do something.

The others watch, listen, try to be there.

Tim Etchells

There's a word for people like you...

Says Richard Lowdon directly addressing those who are watching him near the start of our 1996 performance *Showtime.*

...and that word is... Audience

An audience..., he adds later in the same piece, with much the same attitude of comical menace and accusation *...likes to sit in the dark, and watch other people DO IT.*

This much at least I guess we can count on.

But for the rest it's perhaps for the good that we can't count on much at all.

Theatre and performance are for me best seen as spaces of possibility – places where anything can and should happen. After naturalism, after Brecht, after the absurd, after Kitchen Sink and musicals, after collaborative this and experimental that, after the multi-disciplinary high-and-low-budget, high-and-low-brow extravaganzas, after empty spaces and physical theatres and all that very visual theatre and all that theatre that is also installation and all the performance theatre and the dance drama and the dance theatre and the loud music and the strange slow images and the even-stranger jump-cut images, the re-definition of mime to include talking and the reinvention of dance to more-or-less exclude dancing as such, after all of it, after the fragmentation and the swearing, after the violence and the microphones and the yelling and after the reading and the formal shock horror, after the content *scandale* and the buggery, the no-star reviews and the cacophony of tipping seats, after all that 'is-it-really-acting' and 'is-it-really-theatre' and 'is-it-really-art' etc etc etc perhaps we can say now, finally, that theatre can be what we want and need it to be in order to meet audiences and look them straight in the eyes with a question and an attempt to talk about what it's like to live in this world now. After all that perhaps we can just say that the door is open. That the space is one of possibility – that anything can happen in the next one hour and 45 minutes, that no one needs permission from a parent or guardian or the approval of a responsible adult, the mayor, the Lord Chamberlain or the Ghosts of Shakespeare, Osborne or any living dead critics from any national newspapers, I mention no names. The door is open. Anything is possible. All of the above, and anything more (or less) or anything totally different that anyone feels inspired, inclined or compelled to bring to the table, to the stage. That's all that anyone ever wanted after all; that the door be open and left that way so that more people can get their foot through it, artists and audiences.

So let's do the basics one more time. What are the rules of theatre?

Some people do something. The others watch, listen, try to be there.

Anything else we need to know?

Not really, no.

Are we talking about that old punk adage 'here are three chords now form a band'?

We could be. Or it could be way way more complicated than that. The door is open.

Are we talking about Jasper Johns' three-part instructions piece?

"Take an object.
Do something to it.
Do something else to it".

Sounds good to me. The door is open.

What excites me is work in theatre and performance that makes contact. It might pick people up and really take them places – temporarily making different worlds or states-of-mind, pulling spectators into new landscapes, or incisive re-mixed versions of our own. Or it might just pass on the chance to summon an elsewhere (real or imagined), and take the time instead to draw the people watching into a kind of long and deep look at themselves, even as they sit there in their seats. Either way there's something bold and direct in the work I love, a simplicity and strength that doesn't compromise or contradict its many other much more ephemeral qualities, like risk or fragility or playfulness.

Perhaps the work I see which excites me most combines the approaches above – slipping and sliding between the act of summoning – a story, a world, some figures/'characters', a landscape, a set of concerns – and the process of holding up a mirror to the space and time of the auditorium, inviting the audience to think about itself, its role and place in the world, its role and place in the rather bizarre event or system that is theatre – that strange practice of sitting together in groups of 50 to 1,000, arranged in darkened rows and watching in relative silence while dances, speeches, dialogues or action take place in an area marked out as a stage.

Watching the best theatre and performance we are together and alone. Together in the sense that we're aware of the temporary and shifting bonds that link us both to the stage and to our fellow watchers, plugged into the group around and in front of us, the communal situation, sensing the laughter, attentiveness, tension or unease that grip us collectively, in waves and ripples, in jolts, jumps and uncertain spirals or in other formations that roll and flicker around auditorium and stage, but do not yet have a name. Sat watching we spread out, osmose, make connections. But at the same time, even as we do so, we feel our separateness, our difference from those around us, from those on-stage. Even as we shift and flow with the group, we're aware that our place in its emerging consensus, its temporary community, is partial and provisional – that in any case the group itself – there in the theatre, as elsewhere, in our cities and streets, in the relations between nations, peoples and states – is always as much a fraught and necessary question, a longing and a problem, as it is any kind of certainty.

Nearly twenty years ago, Claire MacDonald wrote that "[t]he media-glutted consumer culture of the city needs a new visual grammar to prise it open," adding that, "[i]f radical theatre really has any future it won't be in a worn-out social realism..."

You could say the same thing now pretty well. The reality moves on – more digital now, more culturally diverse, more nervous, more networked and somehow even more fractured – and as the reality shifts so too theatre and performance duck, dive, shiver and mutate to keep up, shifting and changing in order to grab something of all that takes place, or to contrast it in just the right way, or just to create a space of reflection or refraction that makes just the right kind of sense, or just the right kind of nonsense, and in either case just the right kind of playful intervention, to be true to or true of the time.

For me the places where the action is are those where the door I mentioned before is most emphatically open – those where artists and theatres, makers and venues of different kinds are taking all kinds of risks, taking all kinds of liberties.

Back when Claire MacDonald wrote that article – when Forced Entertainment was all of two years old – we would certainly have been intimidated by a 500-seat theatre, let alone one that contained an audience with much hint of 'the mainstream'. We'd never played in anything like that big, or to that kind of crowd. In those days the ICA, with its 150 or so seats, and the vast expanse of maybe 7.5m width, seemed enormous, official and public in an almost epic way – we'd never really played there either. But by now you could say that things have changed.

For us things changed at first in mainland Europe. I think that's probably very often the case for British artists making theatre outside of the playwriting tradition. A lot of the breaks and chances come from elsewhere. It would have been in Germany or Belgium or Holland that we first played and got used to playing larger spaces, and where we first encountered the larger audiences whose make-up didn't fit the same demographic as those we played to at home. And afterwards Switzerland, Norway, Italy, France, Canada, America and elsewhere. And somewhere in there things changed in Britain too.

For a long time here, at home, we languished in a strange marginal position. Feeling shut-out of larger spaces, locked out of 'the mainstream' (whatever that might be) and at the same time perhaps rather too bound up with the idea of being 'outside', with a self-imposed role of exile, to do much about it. It's telling that the main thing it took to change this situation was a change in our own approach and in our own ambitions. Encouraged by a few strategic programmers, and by a few people inside the funding system, we took to assuming that doors were (or might be) open instead of closed. We got interested in pursuing a dialogue with larger spaces in the UK, seeking out those meetings and conversations where we could talk through plans and ambitions, with an eye towards finding common ground; looking for crossover. And slowly since then, bit by bit, we have found some, in fact more than we might at first have expected.

I get excited about simplicity. About single ideas taken very very far, about approaches pushed to their very limits.

I love work that plugs into popular culture – work which breathes the same air as the rest of us. I love the way that artists sift through almost discarded OR EVERYDAY things – going back through things that are discredited, abandoned or in some sense marginalised by mainstream OR OFFICIAL culture, or by theatre itself. As if here, in the ruins, in the POPULAR FORMS, in the TRACKS, TRACES and detritus of the everyday (sometimes invisible simply because of a certain ubiquity) there might be clues, truths, possibilities. Vaudeville. Magic Acts. Bollywood. Drag. Bad movies, bad TV. Pop songs. Am Dram. Rock gigs. Pantomime. Computer games. Stand-Up. Line Dancing. Musicals. Comic books. These things and others might be relevant in making a theatre for the twenty-first century. Press conferences, show trials, quiz-shows, chat-shows, public inquiries, panel discussions. These might also be relevant. Drag acts, cabaret, storytelling, channel hopping. These might also be relevant. Performance art, poetry, dance, film and visual art. These things might also be relevant. Don't rule anything out. The streets of the city you live in. The fragment of conversation you overheard in a bar. Something your child or your lover whispered when close to edges of sleep. A mis-heard news broadcast. An internet rumour. The door is open after all and the task at hand is to find a theatre that can speak to audiences of the times in which we live.

I get excited about theatre and performance work that is brave enough to surrender control – trusting its audience to think, trusting that they will go to useful places when they're let off the leash of dramaturgical control, or even trusting that a trip through the ostensibly not so useful places (boredom, drifting, free-association) can be more than useful or constructive in the longer run. Trusting audiences, and opening space for them – it's more than one kind of door that needs opening after all.

I get excited about laughter – about the way that a whole audience can start heading that way and I get excited about silence too – about the strange stillness that comes over an audience that is – for a moment, or a whole section – puzzled, conflicted or on tenterhooks because somehow the game has been changed. I love the sudden turns that artists make between laughter and something else – the switch between laughter and silence, or between laughter and tears – and the sudden switch back again.

I love work that shifts me again and again from a recognisable territory – I know where I am – into deeper water, into a place where the references or allusions are more dense, more unclear, or where the combination of things is simply too hard to easily make sense of. The defying of expectations. The breaking of frames. The switch. The jump. The crash. The occasion, in any performance, for sudden wonder.

And I love the way that somehow, whatever its landscape, whatever its means, that the best in contemporary performance brings me back to the world and a consideration of our place in it. The way that the outside comes in, or the inside comes out, unfolding.

Or to put that another way.

Inside the theatre there are only the performers and the audience.

Onstage the performers will have some material items – this night's variation on flimsy or not-so-very-flimsy scenery, plus props, costumes and whatever other stuff. The audience, for their part, will most likely have their coats, their handbags and the contents of their pockets. But *that's all* – aside from the performers, the audience and the stuff they each have with them that's really all there is. *The whole of the rest of the world –* its physical locations and landscapes, its entire population, its complete set of objects and all of its very very many unfolding events, large and small, significant and banal – is invariably outside this room, this place, *emphatically absent.*

Theatre then must always (?) be: the summoning of presence in the context of absence; a bringing in of the world.

And in the space of this – this space of extreme limitation, this space of absurd, almost impossible constriction – anything is possible.

*

Back then in 1986, when Claire wrote that article flagging for the one-millionth time the redundancy of a worn-out-realism, the relationship between the mainstream, the literary theatre and the live art/performance scene in the UK looked very oppositional.

I have to say that writing now, in 2006, it sometimes seems as though things did not change so much. Here in the UK we still do rather too much to deserve a reputation for consuming low-grade American cultural waste-product (I'm talking actors and shows but you can easily extend it to politics) and too much to bolster our image as a kind of quaint museum theme-island with Shakespeare as figurehead stood next to those blokes in the funny outfits at the Tower of London, probably encouraging them to read from *Hamlet* 'just as he first intended it'. Even when things do seem to be moving they don't always move on as much as we'd like to imagine they do. "That British New Writing," one Flemish Theatre programmer said to me years ago, earnestly puzzled or playing devil's advocate, "it's really just the same as the old British writing isn't it?"

Indeed. There are days here when I doubt the depth of the resolve of mainstream theatres to really embrace new approaches, to take bold steps, to really open the door to new work that is produced outside of the literary model, and the new audiences that I think would come with them. And on a larger scale – perhaps more important – there are days when the attitude of suspicion and scepticism in the UK towards art in general – context for the conservatism you can sense in some institutions – gets more than fucking tedious.

But on other days I'm more cheery, though I have to say it's not my natural tendency. I can feel some optimism based on how things already are in mainland Europe, and have been for years, optimism connected to the fact that there is a much

Empty Stages: Ghent
Photo, Hugo Glendinning and Tim Etchells

greater interplay there between 'experimental' theatre and
the mainstream of larger theatres and festivals. I can also
feel optimism because of the strength and persistence of the
alliances that as a company we have made here, on home turf,
and which we've seen other artists make here and there with
larger venues around the country. And I have an optimism
too which arises from the way that British theatre is of course
changing and shifting, not in some monosyllabic way but in fits
and starts, eddies and flurries, especially in the work of groups
and artists from or at 'the edges', artists who are finding new
ways to talk directly and playfully to audiences, new ways to
make theatre and performance speak. I have an optimism too
from the evidence of our own practice, touring here in the UK
– because we've seen many times in different places that when
contextualised properly and marketed with the right kinds of
intelligence and commitment (and resources!) the kinds of work
we make can sit in 'mainstream' venues here, and draw good,
hungry and in the end enthusiastic crowds. It's an optimism
born from the fact that where we do find partners and build
meaningful alliances to present the work (with all the hard work
and effort and struggle to find the way that that implies) – in
Glasgow, in Warwick, in Sheffield, in Dublin, in Newcastle
– that it can and does work. We know this from audience
numbers, from their reactions, from post-show discussions,
from the long emails and other communications we get from
people following shows.

I think audiences grow around what you do and around
what you give them. You get the audience you deserve, or the
audience you expect and conservative programming breeds
conservative audiences. But from my experience here (and
elsewhere) a change of tack can really work. Treat people
like they are intelligent, game for anything, able to cope and
interested in challenging, funny, bright and contemporary art
and they rise to the occasion. There may be some walkouts and

some 'no thank-yous' – but there might very well be along with
that, the beginnings of a relationship with a different audience.
There are plenty of people to whom the words challenging,
experimental, innovative are actually positives, plenty of people
to whom the different take on the world that the so-called
experimental offers is a highly valued addition to their cultural
lives, a useful window on their world. We get to see a lot of
them, at gigs, at home and abroad.

I guess I wasn't asked, in writing this introduction, to outline a
course of action for experimental theatre and the mainstream
– which is just as well since there's too much to be discussed
and tussled over before any such thing could really be resolved
and in any case I doubt that change really comes from policy – I
think it comes from art, and from determined presenters who
want to make things happen. But I do think that it's important
to flag here the need for the funding system to take more
active steps to encourage the larger/mainstream venues in the
UK to make links with experimental theatre, with artists who
are working in different ways, to different agendas. There are
plenty of initiatives and alliances already in existence around
the country that would benefit from this kind of support and
I'm guessing that some financial support might help to make
still more things possible – at least in the sense of taking away
some of the risk that doing new things seems to engender.
I'm wondering too what success in the development of this
area would be? I think if we could look at the programmes of
middle-scale theatres around the country in five years' time
and see innovative projects from experimental theatre-makers
occupying pride of place in the seasons of such venues – not
as opportunistic manoeuvres to fill a split week – but as part of
a serious and ongoing attempt to open doors to new work and

new audiences – then I think we could be sure that the kinds of talks we're having in and around a publication like this one have been worthwhile.

In the meantime of course we'll all just get on with our work, as we always do, venues and artists – making such alliances as we can, finding the best ways to put the strange, darkly comical, ironic, brutal, weirdly entertaining stuff we do in front of audiences because we believe that what we're doing has value and urgency. I'm going to be partisan here as I have been through this writing, not even-handed – I want to say that this work 'outside the mainstream' of which we're just one small part, one tendency in a field of diverse tendencies – this work has for me the most extraordinary capacity to describe, address and engage the contemporary world in vital and vivid terms, and that it reaches audiences with a depth, complexity and clarity that other forms of theatre do rarely these days. Audiences – intelligent, playful, bright and inventive audiences – no matter what you hear to the contrary, are hungry for that. They need and deserve it.

Over the last twenty years I have been working as a performer and director crossing between the worlds of experimental and mainstream theatre. Surprisingly it has been this diversity of influence which I think has made Improbable's work both challenging and POPULAR! In that time it has been essential to let the experimental work feed the work we've done in the mainstream. I learnt as much about tragedy from Rose English and performing at the Comedy Store as I did from directing shows at the Rep theatres. It is essential for the mainstream to acknowledge the debt it has to those working outside the traditional structures and that doesn't just mean giving them a gig and then moving on! It is essential to invest in the process of nurturing the work and develop a muscle for holding that particular space in which this work can grow in.

Phelim McDermott,
Artistic Director, Improbable, 2007

Bringing Glamour To The Masses; The Lyric Hammersmith 1994-2004

Neil Bartlett

Julian Clary in Jean Genet's *Splendid's*,
translated, designed and directed by Neil Bartlett
Lyric Hammersmith, 1995
Photo, John Haynes

Dear Colleagues;

Writing articles about, contributing to discussions on, or just earnestly discussing in foyers this subject of the relationship between 'mainstream' and 'experimental' theatre/performance practice is something that I seem to have been doing fairly solidly since 1982, which is when I first started making what I have always stubbornly called *shows*, and what other people have variously called theatre, experimental theatre, fringe theatre, gay theatre, site-specific theatre, performance art, live art, drag, music theatre, chamber opera, oratorio and even *plays* – depending on where and when they were being performed, and who was watching them and why. However, here we go again...

For the purposes of this letter, I am going to try and give a concise account of some specific, and, I hope salient, ambitions and tactics that were part of a very particular large-scale and long-term project: my work as Artistic Director of the Lyric Hammersmith, a job which I did from 1994 to 2004 in symbiotic partnership with Simon Mellor, who was Executive Director/Producer of the building for that entire period, and without whom nothing much would have happened.

Any orderliness in my account will of course be largely spurious; anyone who downplays the roles of both luck and financial pressure in the achievements of any artistic enterprise – and particularly a building-based one – is more or less lying. Everything that our work at the Lyric did, and didn't, achieve was done under constant and almost-crippling financial pressure, and in the context of the extremely and increasingly competitive and crowded world of London theatre.

Anita Dobson, Guy Dartnell, Amanda Harris and Gregor Trutor in Marivaux's
The Island of Slaves, translated, designed and directed by Neil Bartlett
Lyric Hammersmith, 2002

Before I start to describe some of the things which Simon and I thought and did about this consistently vexed question of the mainstream and the experimental, here are a few points to try and indicate where we were coming from in 1994:

1. Back in 1982, there had been a pretty absolute set of divisions between plays and formally innovative work; between building-based 'theatre' and project-funded touring/arts centre/small-scale 'experimental theatre'; between 'political' work and work which sought to 'entertain.' By 1994, these divisions, it seemed to us, were in meltdown. We were not prepared to be boxed up any longer. This was mostly because...

2. By 1994, I had already tested these divisions to the limit as an artist – I had worked in contexts and venues ranging from the National Theatre and Royal Court at one end (doing a classic eighteenth-century comedy in the former and a radical queer performance musical comedy in the latter) to the National Review of Live Art, the Institute of Contemporary Arts (ICA), derelict warehouses, the Drill Hall, Southwark Cathedral and gay clubs at the other (doing drag, queer devised performance, chamber opera, large-scale experimental music theatre ... categories fail me). In between, I had played just about every arts centre that hosted small-scale touring experimental work in the country. This had been done via the company I was part of, GLORIA.

3. As a gay artist who had started in the 1980s and flowered in the 1990s, I had a very particular take on the division between high and low art, between mainstream and experimental, between popular and precious – the division that dogs every corner of the British creative establishment, and that I personally loathe; to put it simply, I was part of a culture in which such divisions were patently nonsense.

Michael Clark, Fassbinder, Derek Jarman, Frankie Goes to Hollywood, the radical 'powerhouse' regime at the London Coliseum and the glorious, glorious work of the Glasgow Citizens, Philip Hedley's work as producer at Theatre Royal Stratford East – to name but a few of my heroes back in the early days – all made it clear that the journalistic and Arts Council categories of what was formally or politically radical, what was popular, what was 'big' and what was 'small' or 'minor' or 'fringe' were all a bit hidebound and unambitious.

4. If you tour for long enough, you get very tired of re-inventing the wheel, of constantly renegotiating relationships with the performance space, with the technical crew, with the marketing department, with performers, and there are precious few opportunities to build up skills or momentum. And you are always having to constantly renegotiate your funding deals. Most importantly, you have little chance to build up a relationship with an audience, of which more later.

Within those contexts, here are some of the key ways we tried to put our various grievances and ambitions into practice:

1. We dared to assume that the architecture and traditions of the proscenium playhouse – two words that were absolute anathema to most self-appointed radicals in 1994 – might themselves be radical and pleasurable in equal measure. Or, to put it another way, that this might be a site it was worth being specific about. We proposed that having an ambition to play to 500 people night after night for weeks on end (something that in practice we very, very rarely achieved) might be a wonderful thing. That colour, extravagance, theatricality and live music in a night out might be fantastic. That the active, dynamic, intimate relationship between the performer and the audience presupposed by the architecture of a great playhouse like the Lyric might be

something that one should (as manager and producer as well as an artist) try and inculcate in a new generation of young performers, devisers and directors. That the red-velvet-and-gilded-plasterwork cliché might actually be an environment specifically well-suited to inspiring and provoking and supporting transgressive work (if that sounds abstract, then I would quote my own extremist productions of the politically radical costume dramas of Maugham, Rattigan and Genet, not to mention the even kinkier pleasures of rare Marivaux, Kleist and late Shakespeare; the deliriously dotty ideas of inviting Improbable to devise a pantomime or Frantic Assembly or Tamasha to essay actual musicals (physical theatre and music-theatre, they liked to call it – we didn't mind, so long as it was a musical); of inviting Kneehigh to get down and dirty with classic adaptation or Victoria Chaplin to make a kids show). Too often, in our experience, the 'experimental' has been dogged by a nasty taste of Puritanism – by the supposed 'seriousness' and implicit superiority of either new writing or 'performance' and their black-box studio settings – and we were having none of that.

2. There was an unspoken assumption in the late 1980s and early 1990s that 'large-scale' radical work could only be produced on a site-specific basis, or in the context of a festival, or with the protection of an international profile/reputation. While some of these tactics – ones which I had employed myself – were great as stepping stones, it seemed to me very important that the aesthetic and practical, production-skill lessons learnt from the big one-offs were then re-invested in a more continuous, accessible practice. Otherwise, there was a real danger that new British work would retreat into an upward spiral of two-nights-only one-off extravaganzas – high-profile, high-cost, high-class, high-hype but not really providing any working model for change and growth for audiences or performers or funding bodies or venue-based producers.

3. Without telling anyone we were doing it, we responded to the very particular environment of an Edwardian playhouse by foregrounding the visually and physically adventurous – even (especially) when we were doing ostensibly 'literary' plays. This is where we put into practice the lessons we had learnt from all that 1980s so-called 'visual theatre' stuff – Bausch, Lepage, Wooster Group, all the companies who were our peers at the ICA. We achieved this by consistently working with artists of the calibre of (for instance) Rae Smith, Ian McNeil, Robin Whitmore, Paule Constable and Rick Fisher. This meant that over a period of years we were able to gradually erode at the most basic level of what people were actually watching the public perception that plays, literary adaptations, Christmas shows and kids shows were somehow ranked against devised work, physical work and 'multicultural' work in an oppositional hierarchy of theatrical radical-ness versus traditional-ness. Whatever the show, it was never old-fashioned, because it was produced to the highest possible standards by radically minded designers. The old chestnut about visual/physical = radical vs. literary = old-fashioned/boring was gradually eroded. Please note that this took years, was a bloody struggle, and caused great trouble at the box office as audiences and critics and fellow-practitioners have very fixed minds on these matters. They like things in tidy categories. They want to be told what is experimental and what is not.

4. We worked on the assumption that radical work had rights of possession over the main house. Too often, in our touring experience during the 1980s, the studio space attached to a main house was really a guilt-absolving space, where the 'radical' was kept in its place, with small audiences and production budgets; there was no bridge between the two spaces. Therefore, whenever budget constraints allowed, we would identify and hunt down companies who we could

put in the studio specifically in order to initiate a long-term relationship; to introduce a company to the larger culture of the building, the problems and ambitions of larger-scale work; to share skills in production and marketing; to start to build an audience which they could eventually take upstairs with them; to begin to talk to them about how their work would have to grow and develop if it was to move upstairs. This last point is very important; in order for Improbable, Frantic Assembly, Kneehigh, Tamasha and The Right Size and others to make main-house shows, they had to be seduced and inspired into doing that – the work itself has to grow, it can't just be transplanted.

5. We actively sought out places where performers from one tradition could cross over into another. When then-performance-artist Emily Woof proposed a large-scale piece dealing with sexuality, to access an audience of teenage girls, we worked with her on a new staging of *Romeo and Juliet*. We seduced large and various audiences into watching determinedly radical stagings of feminist/queer dramas by casting Joanna Lumley, Sheila Hancock, Maggie Steed, Anita Dobson, Jack Davenport and Julian Clary in them. We smuggled radical non-theatre artistes Neil Tennant, the Ridiculous Theatre's Everett Quinton, Gary Carter, Guy Dartnell, Bette Bourne and Julian Bleach into (respectively) Wilde, Genet, Marivaux, Shakespeare, and a one-night special with Alan Rickman and the Brodsky Quartet. We got people who would never dream of sitting in a proper theatre to come and see The Magnetic Fields, Victoria Chaplin, and The Tiger Lillies – and discover that they were in a great and groovy place. For audiences and artists alike, we actively sought to create a building culture which proposed points of collision and collusion between the 'theatre' and new traditions of performance, rather than division.

6. (And this last point is the Only Thing I Really Care About). The only important difference between 'theatre' and 'experimental theatre/performance', as far as I'm concerned, is that the former takes its audience as a given, whereas the latter is always seeking to extend and challenge and deepen its relationship with the audience, both formally and – most importantly – socially. To put it at its bluntest, main-house theatre looks to the pre-existent audience of the past, new theatre to the audience of the future. Our bright ideas in this department were:

a) All first night performances were free to anyone who lived and worked in the borough. This meant that no one could say that the work wasn't 'for them' – it announced in one stroke that we thought Robert Lepage and Tamasha and Kleist and *Cinderella* staged by Improbable were all equally worthy of their interest (this idea was nicked from Glasgow's Citizens Theatre). It meant that the most surprising people got to see the most surprising things. It sent out a very clear message.

b) We made a lot of noise about there always being one night a week when tickets were dirt cheap, encouraging the idea of experiment and loyalty. Opening doors, not announcing exclusivity.... This idea has since become very popular elsewhere.

c) We put an enormous amount of effort into creating a culture within the building, and then outside the building – in marketing, in press, in the house style, which expressed a determined radicalism and catholicity of taste – no snobbism about (and this is crucial) EITHER the experimental or the mainstream – an abolition of those categories, in effect. I would say this was multiculturalism in its widest sense. Getting audiences used to the idea that they might be sitting next to people NOT like them. (Again, this is a big one as audiences – radical and traditional alike – really don't like things getting too mixed up, specifically class- or age-wise).

d) We put a huge amount of money and effort into our education programme, making it absolutely central to the work and public life of the building, not some guilty or apologetic socially responsible add-on. We realised very early on that it is often artists perceived as 'radical' or 'experimental' who are best placed to create work for younger audiences, and to encourage them to own the building and its shows.

e) At all times and in all places, on every opening night, we asked ourselves this question: WHO IS THIS FOR? WHO IS COMING UP OUR STAIRS?

It was a blast. Perhaps it is as simple as thinking of a theatre-building as a fantastic place, not a problem to be solved.

Yours sincerely,

Neil Bartlett.

Theatre, at its most radically distinctive, is the place where people gather together to invent their future. Consequently, experimentation is its only viable practice: not merely a training ground, not a marginal self-involvement, but theatre fully and faithfully encountering itself in public. It's hard to imagine a more vital optimism.

Chris Goode, 2007

Station House Opera, *Black Works*
Photo, Steve Whitson

Whistling in the Dark

Stella Hall

Why is it that they say of live theatre that one bad experience can put some overly sensitive audience members off for life? In other artforms a woeful gig or yet another Hollywood flop can still see them bouncing back for more. Why don't they take the risk and go back into that darkened room where live performers wait?

I've seen my fair share of indifferent work over the years and there is at least one theatre the pattern of whose upholstery I could, to this day, draw for you blindfold. I sat in agony throughout Peter Brook's *The Ik,* praying for a divine intervention either to make me see what others saw, or to take me away from this corporeal existence. But, with boundless optimism, I still enter those doors each time in hope of transportation of a different kind. Since being taken as a teen to London to see Le Grand Magic Circus at the Roundhouse and Andy Warhol's Marilyns and Campbell's Soup Cans, I have looked for artists who will transport me, out of the here and now, into their world.

I do not believe I am unusual in that, and with a normal human desire for company, I seek to develop audiences who are looking for the same thing. I've worked professionally in that longed-for world over the last twenty odd years in at least seven of our major UK cities, attempting to put together coherent programmes in arts centres and festivals in each, trying to connect with the very different audiences in these different places. I have found audiences in Manchester behave differently from those in Coventry, London, Belfast and now Newcastle Gateshead. Touring artists already know these fine tunings; as audiences we laugh at different things, cough at different moments, remain obstinately silent when a response is anticipated – gasp in the 'wrong' places.

As Peter Sellars once told delegates at the Urban Hymns symposium in Nottingham, 'you have to figure out what an audience wants... and figure out a way to give it to them.' That figuring out takes time. Presenters have to get to know their audience, to feel their pulse, see what works and what doesn't work. That's hellish for the festival director who only gets one go a year, and not so great either for the programmer who needs to roll up her sleeves and go as soon as she arrives at her desk.

In the beginning though, before any 'getting to know you', it's about jumping into that unknown pool and taking the risk, hoping you've got it nearly right and hoping the audience will risk with you. In the past I have lectured on programming and run courses for programmers for the Independent Theatre Council (ITC) with marketeers talking about the marketing mix; rising stars, cash cows, dead dogs (though I've never believed in dead dogs) ... There really is an audience for every performance, you just have to find it, and be truthful while you are at it. I don't believe in easy work and I don't believe in easy answers, but an audience mustn't be deceived or they will never return, and no artist will thank you for misrepresentation. Don't pretend hip hop dancers performing to the occasional tinkling of Tibetan bells is accessible performance for all the family – it isn't. Nor is Karen Finley covering herself in egg yolks and feathers immediately available to any viewer (but those who saw her in The Green Room's opening season knew what they were in for and remember it with as much pride as that select few at the Sex Pistols' first gig). For a presenter, there is nothing as satisfying as seeing that invisible bond between an audience who have come through a challenging show together.

If it doesn't work and they don't even turn up (a risk that is built into every programming decision) you can console yourself by saying it was an idea before its time. In my first year at the Belfast Festival I sat with 40 people in a 300-seat auditorium watching Victoria from Ghent present their miraculous production of *Ubung*. Performers aged twelve to sixteen voiced their badly behaving adult counterparts on a silent film projected onto a downstage screen. It spoke movingly and with the lightest touch of how we adults influence a child's development. I now realise it was too early to present that show; we had not grown the audience for it. Two years later, after a major audience development programme, we could have filled those seats, but I still believe it was a risk worth taking.

Freudian psychoanalysts at the turn of the twentieth century concluded it was not normal to overcome natural fears at all, and that risk-taking behaviour was evidence of a diseased mind. Fortunately for us twenty-first centurions that is no longer widely held to be true! Contemporary thinkers say that although some people are undoubtedly 'riskier' than others, we have evolved as a species to take risks in order to survive. Certainly I don't believe programmers can survive without risk, and with risk comes the possibility of failure. We need long range goals to keep us from short range failures and for me, that goal is all about finding ways to introduce beautiful and challenging work to audiences, and finding partners in passion with whom to do it.

In 1983 Jeremy Shine and I co-founded The Green Room in Manchester. It was the first multi-artform venue in the city and funds had been set aside by the departing Greater Manchester Council for its establishment. The owners of the first venue we chose – an amateur dramatic club – mislaid the title deeds and we were forced into a wandering life, promoting events in a host of different places. Happily, it was the basis for a philosophy of partnership that hasn't changed since.

We worked together with all the venues in the city, matching artists to locations. Trickster flew from the steel tubing of the Royal Exchange, we presented the Institute of Contemporary Arts' (ICA) *Performing Clothes* with Leigh Bowery at the Hacienda, Impact Theatre strutted their beautiful stuff in *The Carrier Frequency* at the Royal Northern College of Music and we heaved Lumiere and Son's sets down the steep steps to the Library Theatre stage. In Didsbury, drama students walked out after a day's rehearsal as we got shows in. I wanted to grab them by the hair and yank them back, saying 'look what you're missing!' But they were going on to be different kinds of theatre-makers, or television actors, and didn't connect with what we thought to be some of the finest artists of our age: Hesitate and Demonstrate, Forkbeard Fantasy, IOU (who I really believed had dug down to another realm below the stage), People Show, Station House Opera – some introduced by Artsadmin, a key partner over the years, some identified directly. We staged Forced Entertainment's second show, *Nighthawks*, in 1985 in the basement of the Adult Education Centre on Oxford Road, the beginning of a long and fruitful relationship which would go on to the commissioning of *Dreams' Winter*, a site-specific work for Central Library. LIFT began life in 1981 and in 1983 we jointly programmed MIFT (an unfortunate acronym!) beginning a partnership which saw international work regularly visiting the city over the years.

Finally in 1989 we opened our own venue under the railway arches in Whitworth Street, sleeping there on the nights before opening since the alarms weren't working and frankly we couldn't bear to be away. Home at last to all those touring companies who had slummed it in Birch Community Centre or the Brickhouse, Contact's very basic studio, and home to the countless artists growing up in Manchester: Doo Cot, Whalley Range Allstars, New Breed, The Glee Club, Rivca Rubin and Michael Mayhew. All of these made it a place of shared ideas and experiment.

New companies and artists emerged from the old: Steve Shill, Graeme Miller, Heather Ackroyd, Alison Andrews. And work from Gary Stevens, Bobby Baker, Dogs in Honey, Gay Sweatshop, Improbable, motiroti, desperate optimists and DV8 were part of the roll call. So were Women's Theatre Group, Them Wifies, Mrs Worthington's Daughters, and Black Theatre Co-operative. The Green Room was part of a national circuit, with Neil Wallace and Janek Alexander at Chapter in Cardiff; Michael Morris then Lois Keidan and Catherine Ugwu at the ICA; Nikki Milican at Midland Group, Nottingham, then the Third Eye Centre; and a small group of others who kept each other informed and buoyed up when it began to seem like a huge burden to be running a building, when so much exciting work was happening well outside traditional boundaries.

But what was this? The world music audiences, which had been so plentiful at the Royal Northern College of Music (RNCM), didn't want to come in such numbers to The Green Room, and narrative theatre work, so successful when presented by us in the Library Theatre, didn't fare as well either. What next? The producing theatres would be programming the work themselves, taking bread from the mouths of honest arts centres! And they did. The audiences behaved differently in different venues too, and that's not just because they were a different group of people – there was obviously an overlap, but because the context had changed and the new location shaped the perception of an audience as to its relative merits and value. So, work presented in a funky railway arch had its context shaped for it in the same way as work presented in the hallowed surroundings of the Royal Exchange, the region's premier theatre.

Despite our much vaunted commitment to partnership, it was at first another matter when what we saw as our role was being usurped. We really thought the reps should stick to producing plays and let us do the rest. It seems foolish now; the world has changed and few theatres can afford, or desire, to produce year round. But such was the sense of separation at the time that few theatres chose to invite experimental touring work in for other than financial reasons. It certainly wasn't initially a passion for the work.

However, there were exceptions, and these grew, year on year. People like Neil Bartlett took on the Lyric Hammersmith, Ruth Mackenzie went to Nottingham Playhouse. A new generation of theatre-makers were introducing diversity in a way that has changed the face of our building-based companies ever since.

Meanwhile, Stephen Daldry invited me in to run the annual Barclays New Stages Festival at the Royal Court Theatre. This scheme provided new funds to make experimental work and was a truly welcome addition to the limited support available through the Arts Council. For several years I worked with an impressive marketing team who cross-sold Rose English, Stan's Café, NVA, Ralf Ralf, Semblance, Forced Entertainment and a host of others to audiences who thought that what they really wanted was the English Stage Company and new writing but decided that they would take a little risk. Who cared if the Royal Court's initial motivation was financial and that Barclays paid for us to present work during the difficult summer months? We were able to commission Pete Brooks with the Islington Festival and Bobby Baker with the Chelsea Physic Garden. It was an arranged marriage with benefits to all. The programme raised the profile of artists who would never have appeared in those surroundings otherwise. Candoco were the first disabled artists to appear on that stage, and motiroti the first Asian company. The partnership with LIFT continued and a new one, with Pride, began. We co-presented Edward Lam and the Handsome Foundation, helping the Royal Court build new audiences for their commission to Lloyd Newson of DV8.

Sadly, not all experiments work out. Barclays took advice from others with different agendas and, despite protests, decided to put their funds into slightly less challenging middle-scale touring work. One or two of the companies had in fact been unsuited to that confining stage, and unhappy with the attitudes to artists from a fine art or live art background of some technicians steeped in West End practices. Negative, unwelcoming, some practised a level of separatism that exemplified all that was worst in what Barry Rutter often described as 'velvet theatre'. Some, but by no means all. Bad old habits die hard, and no doubt they are still on display in the deepest reaches of theatres where one dare not mention Macbeth, nor whistle.

Thankfully, these attitudes were not in evidence at Warwick Arts Centre where I joined a devoted team including the current director Alan Rivett to deliver a huge range of events. Here, the great pleasure of working with a curator of the skill and knowledge of Sarah Shalgosky enabled real linkages between performance, live art and the visual arts to be made. Lois Keidan assisted on developing a fledgling live art programme which I am proud to say still continues thanks to partnerships with Mark Ball of Fierce.

There were different challenges in Northern Ireland. An earlier Festival Director had described the Belfast Festival at Queen's as 'neutral', and indeed to be successful, many events there must take place in neutral locations. But art is anything but neutral; it must engage, and I therefore set out to find an active engagement with a range of cultural communities. It didn't work with *Ubung,* but in partnership with the Ormeau Baths Gallery, the Old Museum, and the Lyric Theatre – all looking to build new relationships with audiences – many new experiences happened. Quarantine guided blindfolded audiences through *Something a Taxi Driver in Liverpool Said,* Improbable brought *Sticky* to 7,000 people from all backgrounds and Pure Movement connected young people from both sides of the divide. However, mistakes continued: in 2001, I was naively unprepared for sectarianism to flare up at the invitation to a young Israeli dance troupe to perform. Petitions against it were written, signed by local artists participating in the Festival, and demonstrations took place outside the venue as audiences ran the gauntlet of photographers from the *Andersonstown News.* Several members of the nationalist community made political capital out of the visit which we refused to cancel, unwilling to penalise artists for the views of the government under which they laboured. It was a difficult time, and demonstrated only too clearly the need to wait and listen, get to know a place and figure out what the audiences there really need.

I'm now in a place where yet another generation are doing the figuring out, and getting better at it all the time. Erica Whyman at Northern Stage is inviting artists to process into her new building and construct castles in the air outside it, and John McGrath at Contact Theatre is bringing in an audience who once would simply have kicked a ball against the outside wall.

Edison did sixteen hundred experiments before he invented the light bulb. When a friend asked why he was wasting so much time and not achieving anything he answered that of course he'd accomplished something – he'd learnt 1,600 ways it doesn't work! Over the years I must have made at least sixteen hundred mistakes but one has to keep moving forward. Fear is false expectations appearing real and fear of failure can be a paralyzing thing. It can make us take the easy route, or not even go on the journey. But, as Peter Sellars wrote, 'probably some of the most awesome and beautiful and powerful things we can do will fail.'

All Graeae's work is intrinsically experimental theatre. Experimental theatre in the UK is seen as a dare or a risk. All creative endeavour is a risk with experimentation as the heart beat. This gives artists the adrenalin to cut the edges of anal traditionalism. UK artists rely on this buzz because let's face it not all of us are in it for the money! Experimental theatre needs to be embraced and not seen as something that only resides within college walls otherwise our theatrical climate will continue to be a series of white middle-class kitchen sink dramas playing to the same audiences forever and ever.

Jenny Sealey, Artistic Director, Graeae Theatre Company, 2007

As Natural as Breathing

John E McGrath

SKID 180
Photo, Joel Chester Fildes

A few months ago I had the opportunity to see a work in progress by a talented emerging artist who had first become involved in Contact as a participant in our young people's programmes over six years ago. This young artist had made a solo show about the relationship between a young black man in Manchester and his Jamaican father, and the performance was a moving and sometimes disturbing portrayal of life in today's Britain.

Watching the show, though, what impressed me wasn't just the raw, honest subject matter, but the confident, experimental form in which it was presented. Without needing to flash any deconstructive angst around, the performance integrated an impressive and thoughtful range of approaches to theatre into an edgy, self-aware whole.

Afterwards I had a chat with the young theatre-maker who had created the piece, and admitted to him that while I'd been expecting to be impressed by his work – as I knew how talented he was – I'd been surprised at his confidence in experimenting with form. He laughed and told me that he'd learned a lot in all of the workshops he'd done at Contact, but that probably one of the most transformative things he'd done with us was take a job as an usher. While earning five pounds an hour each night for two years, he'd sat in the theatre watching everyone from Forced Entertainment to Benji Reid, from Quarantine to The Builders Association and motiroti. When he came to make his own work, he found all of these theatrical languages pumping through his blood. Experiment was as natural to him as breathing.

Contact is a theatre space dedicated to new performance and to young people. With participation at the core of everything we do, and a 'ninety-nine per cent new work on stage' policy, we have developed a theatre-making environment that differs radically from the models both of regional producing theatre and of the presenting arts centre. Every day at Contact, new work is being made. Sometimes this is a play with a writer and a director and a cast of Equity actors, sometimes it is a group of emerging artists in a residency together. Sometimes it is ambitious new work with young people, often working alongside some of the most exciting contemporary practitioners, from Belgium's Victoria to Manchester's Quarantine. But because this daily business of making work is done in such a variety of ways, its outcomes can also be very various. There will be weeks when every space in the building – from theatres, to rehearsal room, to foyers – are all filled with artists showing new work they have made in the building. Other times a whole month may go by with only one or two performances of work that has developed inside Contact.

With a wide-ranging programme of workshops and residencies always in full swing, it would be quite possible to run Contact as a space that opened its doors to an audience only on the occasions when we had created a new piece of work. We would certainly still have plenty to keep us busy. And in some ways this would seem to fit our core focus of new performance and young people. However, there is a whole other aspect to what we do, which sits alongside these developmental activities, and informs them in a vital way: our programme of visiting work.

As well as the work that we produce with artists and young people in the building, Contact presents a busy programme of new work from visiting companies. Some of these companies have a long relationship with us, and have become partners with whom we collaborate on a regular basis. Others may simply be artists who we feel are doing something exciting, and whose work we would like to share with our audiences. The programme includes work by a huge range of companies. Many of them produce 'experimental theatre'.

We see the artists and companies who visit us as intrinsic to the creative life of our theatre. We try to provide as welcoming and as social a space as possible, not just because we want to be nice, but because we hope that these visiting artists will relax enough to spend time with the artists and young people around and about the building. We want them to leave ideas, opinions and techniques behind, to leave us changed in some way.

Of course, workshop programmes, outreach projects, audience development initiatives can all be part of this work, and with our audience primarily under 35 years old, we are competing with a lot of other attractions to gain their attention and loyalty. But all the marketing initiatives in the world can't begin to approach the effect of a young performer from Lonsight, Rusholme, Moss Side, or Moston accidentally ending up in a discussion with an experimental performance artist from Holland or New York, as both wait for the kettle in the green room to boil, or as they find themselves sharing the same table in the bar.

To separate 'experimental theatre' out as needing different study or skills – something that both the education system and the funding bodies are often keen to do – is to forget that for artists, and for young people, experiment should be as natural as breathing. While a substantial conservative theatre audience may well want its drama served in a recognisably 'well-made' dish at a realistically-rendered, period-appropriate dining table, or delivered by a well-spoken ensemble of attractive RADA-trained all-rounders, for the majority of the population all theatre is an experiment, a leap of faith, a rarity.

At Contact, the single programming choice that most strikes fear into our marketing staff is a piece of well-made drama. This isn't to say that we don't take the risk, and when a company, such as Paines Plough, has a reputation for consistently high-quality, provocative work, the audiences will come, and come back. But in general for our young audiences, the biggest fear is that theatre will be boring. Forced Entertainment, Quarantine, Company F.Z, motiroti, may be challenging, strange, difficult and sometimes even annoying, but they are very rarely dull. And so we can programme them with confidence, and people will come: young people, from a range of backgrounds, for a range of reasons. Some of them will walk out before the end. Others will come back next time and bring their friends.

A successful theatre director once complimented me on the niche we had built at Contact. It was meant as a compliment, but I took it as a challenge. 'We don't have a niche', I replied. 'You have the niche. In the so-called mainstream houses, with their subscriber audiences, the same few thousand people turning up again and again. That's the niche. We have everyone else!'

Of course, I was lying. We have a good number of people coming to Contact, and many of them go away with a fair bit of theatrical experiment in their blood. But there's a whole lot more people still to reach. What I am absolutely convinced of is that they will never be reached by the kind of theatre that is habitually described as mainstream. Commercial theatre may find a lot of them: good spectacle will always have a role. But the kind of stodge that is served up as well-made theatre in subsidised venues will only ever play to a minority crowd.

The dichotomy between experimental and mainstream benefits no one, it marginalises one side and fossilises the other. Good theatre is always an experiment. And the way to find audiences is to invite them, in an enjoyable way, to share in the experiment.

So, at Contact, we attempt to create an open, exploratory environment, which is as accessible and engaging to a sixteen-year-old from Cheetham Hill as it is to a fifty-year-old performance art legend from New York City. And by and large it works. Figures such as New York's Penny Arcade return to Contact with glee because they can meet people they would never meet in more rarefied experimental environments. And any artist worth their salt knows that running into the same bunch of people on the same international or national circuit can never be good for the creative soul.

We avoid, where possible, over-categorising work. We don't have a main house or a studio programme – when you book a show, we don't tell you what space it is in until you arrive. We try to avoid over-segmenting our marketing. Yes we may send you a flier for The Builders Association if you came to the recent Forced Entertainment show, but we may send you information on Benji Reid, or a new club night, or the artist residency programme too.

We don't have a subscriber audience. We battle for every audience member for every show. Sometimes our efforts may work better than others, but we are never stuck with trying to fulfil the expectations of a single core group.

We involve our audience in our programming. Through our Action Contact project, audience members can become involved in developing the programme, going out to see work, feeding back on proposals for shows, and evaluating the work we put on. A feisty, committed group of young programmers regularly surprises me with their tastes, and often guesses the audience response better than I do.

Just as we put participation at the heart of everything we do, so we encourage experiment at all levels. Our workshop programmes are all developed as artistic experiments, trying out something new. We train artists from a truly diverse range of backgrounds – in terms of artform, culture and experience – to develop work with young people. And we support them properly. Many artists, particularly with experimental companies, have had bad experiences in the past on poorly managed projects, often being asked to work alone, or with inappropriate groups. We try to match artists and young people in a thoughtful if challenging way. We want both sides to come out wanting to do this again!

We ask workshop artists to work in new teams, to surprise and learn from each other, at the same time as challenging participants.

We provide a wide range of 'emerging artist' programmes, where participants can start to define themselves as artists, where young artists can come and work with us for the first time, and where more established artists can change gear or try something new. We set these up in structures where interaction and shared learning will be at the heart of things.

Like all experimenters, sometimes we fail. There have been shows that next to no one has come to. There have been participatory projects that have seemed radical, but have produced predictable, unexciting work. There have been residencies that have been unsatisfying or unhappy. When these things happen, we try to learn something, because the only bad experiment is one that teaches you nothing.

And sometimes we succeed gloriously. Such as the time we won an award and decided that the prize money should be spent on asking two artists who had never worked together to make an experimental theatre piece with any young people from Contact they wanted to choose. The only rule was that the show should be called *Manchester*. I'd expected something unusual, but probably full of Manchester energy: the music, the clubs, the street style. The mysterious, meditative installation that Juliet Ellis and Craig Conway developed with six of Contact's young people (a couple of whom had, just a few years ago, been among the most 'challenging' of our participants) was wonderfully, disturbingly, like nothing I had imagined. These young performers had developed a style of performance so subtle, suggestive and strange, that you felt like you were being taken into a world where the rules existed only for this moment, and only in their hands. Experiment had become as natural to them as breathing.

So, I suspect that experimental theatre will thrive most in our venues when we accept that all theatre must be an experiment, and that there can be accessible, funny, engaging experiments, just as there can be challenging, difficult, disturbing experiments. When we stop trying to explain experiment to audiences and instead listen to them explaining their reactions to us. When we market each show on its unique characteristics, and not on some judgement as to who ought to like it. When we stop trying to amuse the same few people every week, and go out and find some new people. When we allow experimental artists to inhabit venues, not just visit them on sufferance now and then. And when we embrace the many young theatre artists for whom experiment is a natural, enjoyable, everyday way of looking at the world.

I can
recommend
the ride!

Alan Rivett

I remember the moment well. It was as if a coming of age ritual. Nothing was said, just a look – to share and to read on another's face.

Standing at the back of Warwick Arts Centre's steeply raked 550 seat theatre with Tim Etchells of Forced Entertainment, ready for the start of a performance of *First Night* in October 2001 with a full house extending all around us. This was the culmination of many years of hard work by a lot of people making new work and the shared look was the summing up, neither triumphant nor overindulgent, more of a realisation that this was probably quite an important moment for both of us. The fact was that after twenty years of passion for experimental work, squeezed into studio spaces, not being able to programme everything every time, losing productions to Europe, taking on doubt, guilt, moving on from difficult conversations without resolution, here we were with a full main house for a Forced Entertainment show!

Marisa Carnesky, *Carnesky's Ghost Train*
Photo, courtesy the artist

But where had we come from to arrive here? I'm sure part of the answer lies in the idea of an 'Arts Centre'; a place where mainstream and experiment can cohabit and, in the minds of many, should cohabit. I have been inclined to reject the idea of the 'mainstream' as dominant cultures always evolve. I well remember the moment when radical left-wing theatre company Belt and Braces arrived in the West End with Dario Fo's *Accidental Death of an Anarchist*. For those of us working in community theatre at the time this was not just a confirmation that the mainstream was evolving but an affirmation that what we were engaged in, experiment with form and content, would inherit the mainstream! So let's not be prescriptive in our descriptions and categorisation (leave this to the bureaucrats).

Warwick Arts Centre, since opening in 1974, has maintained a programme of work by experimental artists. This has waxed and waned over the last thirty years depending on the interests of the Arts Centre Director and the nature of work being made. Artists and companies such as IOU, Bobby Baker, Station House Opera and Forced Entertainment had an established (though erratic) part of Warwick Arts Centre's programme during the 1990s. The experimental/ live art programme was given a significant lift on the arrival of Stella Hall as Director in 1998. Stella, a lifetime champion of experimental work, nurtured from her founding of Manchester's Green Room, put this strand of programming firmly into the organisation's consciousness. Serious collaboration with the Fierce Festival, consistency of programming, linking to UK and international live art networks and talking to live and experimental artists became the norm. The list of artists and companies playing to sizeable audiences grew: Goat Island, Franko B, Ron Athey, Gob Squad, Ursula Martinez, Marisa Carnesky and Kazuko Hohki all took their part in the programme, most, more than once and will continue to do so. Why? Because (and this is surely up for debate) as a multidisciplinary arts centre I believe we have a responsibility to artists to nurture their work and provide a platform for it.

What about audiences? We have a responsibility to them too, but if audiences' interest in experimental work is negligible then it's really not worthwhile either for the organisation or the artists. Finding and encouraging audiences to experience experimental work thus becomes part of our job. This isn't so different to other parts of Warwick Arts Centre's programme. We work at exposing classical music audiences to Bruckner, Messiaen, Birtwistle and Adams; so what's the difference in approach in introducing audiences to Station House Opera and Gob Squad? Well, context is everything. Warwick Arts Centre exists in a university where students study performance; it exists in the West Midlands with a population of over three million people; it partners with Fierce, an annual festival of experimental performance; there are University and FE lecturers leading their students to an appreciation of experimental performance; and the practice of companies such as Forced Entertainment and DV8 are included for study on Post-16 exam course curricula. Though a minority interest, it is clear that sufficient enthusiasm exists for experimental work to attract audiences alongside the mainstream. There is a twin track approach which goes some way to securing the successful outcome of a well-attended performance for experimental work:

1. consistency of programming
2. knowing and tracking 'champions' among the potential audience

Simply slotting an appearance by a live or experimental artist or company into a season and then forgetting about this programme for another year will lead to tears. Audiences need to know that the organisation is serious about experimental work to give it a coherent and consistent presence. Artists also need the assurance that they are not always being asked to be 'trailblazers' with nothing to follow.

'Champions', teachers, lecturers, other artists (to name a few) need nurturing, forward notice, to be listened to and taken notice of. They are the conduits to larger numbers of like-minded people who will, if treated well, bring other audiences with them.

Let's not be over optimistic though. Consistency and care for champions takes time and will. These are so easily over-ridden by any number of pressing issues which arise in most venues most of the time: financial imperatives, reluctance to take too many risks with the programme, and political interference.

All the above accepted, experimental work continues to be largely locked into studio-sized dimensions in both gallery and performance space. The exception is grand site-specific work, largely too expensive and complex for a venue to take on.

Our case study of Marisa Carnesky's *Ghost Train* and the Clod Ensemble's *Red Ladies* suggests that nothing is impossible given strong powers of persuasion and enduring partnerships (as well as a healthy dose of bloodymindedness).

There are three specific contributing factors to the success of these extraordinary events:

1. a time specific/political need for Warwick Arts Centre to reposition itself in relation to Coventry as a city, its citizens and the political decision-makers

2. Coventry, as a location in the West Midlands sharing in a major way in the region-wide Fierce Festival
3. the ability to form real partnerships to assist delivery

Fierce and Warwick Arts Centre had maintained a well-articulated interest in Marisa Carnesky's *Ghost Train* since hearing the initial idea. This matured fairly quickly into a joint financial contribution as co-commissioners. At the same time a separate and specific campaign was underway to convince opinion formers in Coventry that Warwick Arts Centre was a 'part of the City's cultural infrastructure' to counter arguments that as an 'out of town university based facility', Warwick Arts Centre had little relevance to the people of Coventry. *Ghost Train* was the perfect vehicle to demonstrate in a palpable way that Warwick Arts Centre and Fierce Festival had a genuine place in Coventry and for Coventry people all that was needed was a partnership to assist in the delivery of a complex and intricate project. CV One, Coventry's unique and skilled city centre management company, were the perfect partners. CV One provided all on-site logistical support, utilities, equipment hire services and licensing. Warwick Arts Centre maintained overall project management responsibility, with Fierce Festival providing all 'front of house' on-site personnel. *Ghost Train*, which had had a somewhat chequered life up to the point of arrival in Coventry in May 2005, operated like a dream for a week during Fierce '05. It performed to 100% audience capacity, developed creatively under Marisa's guidance during its visit to Coventry and received very positive audience feedback.

The *Red Ladies* project, under the creative direction of the Clod Ensemble, has just happened in Coventry. Drawing on the *Ghost Train* experience, our objective was to secure partners in Coventry, perform the work entirely in Coventry to a Coventry and Fierce audience. It didn't work as planned! City centre space became unavailable, logistical support for the kind of event envisaged was seen as uncertain and the decision was made to revert to a daily *Red Ladies* mission in the city centre and an evening performance (involving 22 Red Ladies!) at Warwick Arts Centre. Again, in collaboration with Fierce '06, the *Red Ladies* project worked well for us.

Warwick Arts Centre has maintained a distinct policy, as an arts centre, of presenting the work of mainstream and experimental artists. This policy has been sustained and given the organisation a unique programme with broad appeal.

Keys to success are not for the fainthearted, demanding above all the desire to take risks and not abandoning programming experimental artists when the going gets tough. Audiences need consistency of programming and clear communication, especially with trailblazers / live art ambassadors.

The benefits are enormous. New artistic horizons, engaging performers and creators, excitement within the organisation about the extraordinary nature of some experimental work as well as press and TV attention for some of the more eyecatching work.

I can recommend the ride!

All kinds gather, a place
of provocation, a challenge to
both the artist and their audience.
An exciting possibility.
A bridge is built reflecting our own
contradictions, in the bridging –
a process of transformation –
these opposite forces connect
and reflect our human existence.
This is an act of artistic creation.
This becomes the reality.
Juliet Ellis, 2007

Growing
Audiences

Veteran theatre PR Mark Borkowski, and the co-founders and former directors of the London International Festival of Theatre (LIFT), Rose Fenton and Lucy Neal, in conversation with journalist Brian Logan about the role of marketing in growing audiences for experimental theatre.

Graeme Miller, *A Girl Skipping*
Photo, Bob Van Dantzig

Brian Logan (BL)
Can you start by introducing your general principles of theatre marketing and publicity?

Mark Borkowski (MB)
Theatre is about changing people's lives. It's about exciting people. That's why I do this job. For me, as an individual with Polish roots, my greatest theatre experience was seeing *The Dead Class* by Tadeusz Kantor. This was in the 1970s, and I schlepped over to Riverside Studios to see it. Why? I was curious to discover what it was about. So I went, and I just couldn't believe what I saw. For days, there were images of that show in my mind. I thought: well, I'm touched by that, and I could easily never even have seen it. How less rich my life would have been!

Theatre marketing is about communicating that passion. Anybody who I work for, anybody who pays me a fee, knows that I am passionate about the work. Knows that I totally get their vision. And it becomes a mission for me, to take their work out there and get as many people as possible to see it. So that others can have the same feeling that I did when I saw Kantor. If a publicist hasn't got that kind of passionate commitment, if they're just doing a job for you – well, forget it.

To me, the essential questions that underpin theatre marketing are: what is interesting about the work? What are the visual pictures that will sell it, that will distil its impact? Who are the people likely to be excited by it, outside the traditional arts ghettoes? And answering these questions helps us create word-of-mouth. That's what theatre publicity is about.

BL
Is there scepticism towards marketing within theatre and the arts?

The theatre critic Michael Coveney wrote in his book that I was evil for bringing modern marketing practises into theatre. Traditionally, theatre publicity was by rote: you got listings, you brought in a photographer for the previews, then you got the critics in. Job done. And there is still a tendency to think that the review is all, that you're working towards the review. But the review is not all. The journey leading up to it is in itself very exciting. And crucial to the marketing of a production.

But theatre people aren't always sympathetic to that. I remember going to see an experimental theatre company in the East End of London, years and years ago. And the Artistic Director said to me, 'I've got to talk about marketing, because the Arts Council and the British Council and all the other funding bodies don't think we get enough audiences.' And I said, 'what do you mean?' And he said, 'well, we do it for our mates, really. If we get two people, that's good enough for us.' And I thought: how small an aspiration is that? But a lot of that old brigade felt that their primary duty was to the audience that were already committed to them.

So in the theatre, the publicist is usually the last person brought into the process. And by the time you're given the material, maybe you've only got three weeks to make it work. It's not enough. At the moment, I'm helping David Jubb, Artistic Director at Battersea Arts Centre (BAC) with an idea – and we've already been talking about it for two years.

BL

Could you talk about the specific challenges posed by marketing experimental performance? And can you relate that to your experiences working with LIFT?

MB

First of all, I don't think marketing experimental theatre is essentially different from marketing mainstream theatre. What you've got to look at is still: is the show good, or is it going to be good? That's really the only consideration.

BL

So, in terms of marketing, you don't see any reason why mainstream venues should be nervous of programming experimental work?

MB

No I don't.

Rose Fenton (RF)

I don't think mainstream venues are nervous anymore of alternative performance. In recent years, the major institutions have squatted on the ground of the fringe. The Barbican has the likes of Duckie and the artists William Yang and Richard Maxwell performing there. These are huge changes. There's even a case for saying experimental theatre has gone too mainstream, insofar as the media may now say to themselves: it's easy to hear about Bobby Baker, or the next generation of Bobby Bakers, through the Barbican and the National Theatre, rather than going out on a limb to some unknown, newly-emerging organisation.

In any event, I think labels are dangerous. LIFT never sold itself as a festival of experimental theatre. We just said, 'this is amazing work from around the world, which will take you on an adventure, theatrically.' And that's how Mark led people into it.

MB

There's one sense in which contemporary performance is actually easier to sell. Because most of these companies are collectives of people with a vision, and with a real commitment to making their work. Look at Archaos: a collective of people together. The Jim Rose Circus: a collective of oddballs together. That's very important. The commitment of these people is their power. So marketing becomes about channelling that single-mindedness. The problem comes when that collective spirit becomes isolationist. Certain artists think 'the world is against us, they don't understand.' Better to think: we want the world to understand us. You need to understand and to find the types of people that will appreciate your work.

RF

When we first brought over De La Guarda – an unknown company, with no track record anywhere apart from Argentina – how did you sell them? What was your approach there?

MB

I travelled to Bordeaux to see De La Guarda, knowing nothing about the company. They performed in a nuclear submarine workshop. You went down, down, down into this room, which was dark like I'd never seen dark before. And silent like I'd never heard before. And then this performance happened. It was ecstasy. It was like a hallucinogenic drug. From that point onwards, a power and responsibility are passed onto you, to say 'I am determined to let everybody else experience what I've experienced.' Basically, that entails telling people, to their faces: 'you will enjoy this.'

That face-to-face communication is important. I used to have an office in Clerkenwell, and I used to take a handful of press releases across the road to the *Guardian*. And I would just walk in and talk to people. Publicity is about that connection. If you look people in the eyes and they can actually see or hear your enthusiasm, they get curious.

Lucy Neal (LN)
You arranged a press trip to Argentina for De La Guarda. That was quite shocking to us at the time, because LIFT's budget was not big – but you chose to invest our money in sending journalists overseas to see work in advance. Nowadays that's taken for granted. I was fascinated to read recently that Michael Billington had visited India – where he'd never been before – to see Tim Supple's *A Midsummer Night's Dream*. And his review a few weeks later was qualitatively different, because he, as a human being, had engaged in the process of the making of the work.

In LIFT's case these trips were essential for the added reason that they led to preview articles. Our artists were often here for two or three days only, so we could never rely on reviews to sell tickets. Whatever coverage we received had to be something that captured people's imaginations at an earlier stage.

RF

Another benefit of the press trip is that it enables the participating writers to talk about the wider context: where is this work coming from? In Buenos Aires, post-dictatorship, there was a real sense of anarchy and questioning as a younger generation was making themselves heard. De La Guarda told us, 'we don't trust words anymore. We want to express ourselves through creating a new reality.' So with press trips, you can convey to your audience the context in which this work has happened.

MB

The key to press trips, and to promotion in general, is that you've got to find people who'll be interested. I have always, and I still do, read every newspaper every day. And what I have an ear for is, 'that writer might be interested in this.' It's about finding journalists with curious, interesting minds, regardless of their discipline, and matching them to the productions they might be interested in. Where things go wrong is if you just go, 'he is a theatre critic, let's send him.' You have to understand what these people are writing. Understand what they're interested in. And if they're not, don't force a square peg into a round hole.

But the publicist must go further. Why do art and entertainment have to get stuck in a ghetto? Why do they have to go on the arts pages? My mission has always been: how do you get work out of the ghetto and onto the pages where the most people are likely to see it?

LN

The thing I remember in terms of fresh approaches to getting audiences is that we worked with the Catalan artist, Alberto Vidal, whose LIFT'85 performances took place in London Zoo. Mark got Alberto onto the Terry Wogan show, which was a piece of live art in itself, and a genius piece of PR for his show.

MB

Alberto Vidal was a real battle, because when it came to marketing, London Zoo didn't want to know. My trick was to take a *Daily Telegraph* journalist called Byron Rogers along with me to a meeting at London Zoo. And he talked to the Zoo's director about how this was going to be the front page of the *Telegraph* magazine. That's how they started to recognise that this would be a big draw. Twenty thousand extra people went to London Zoo because of Vidal's show.

RF

I remember, Mark, every time we sat down to talk about an upcoming festival, your first question would always be: where are the images?

MB

One of the things I was noticing back then was the growing power of the image. There was more and more space for photos in newspapers. One of my first jobs was with a contemporary dance company. I sat down one day with them and said: 'the ideas you're coming up with, they'd make great pictures. Why don't you work with a photographer?' And they ummed and aahed and said, 'but we don't know what the show is going to be.' I encouraged them to introduce a photographer into their process, and the photos would help define the work, potentially. We got a part-photographer, part-artist called Holly Warburton and she created these amazing pictures. And magazines like *ID* and *The Face*, who hadn't seen theatre photos before, were running them across half-pages. I thought: we're onto something here. It's about distilling theatre – particularly visual theatre, and the types of theatre that have language barriers – into great images.

LN

I remember, Mark, images you got into *Elle* magazine. In the Nineties, LIFT commissioned five new pieces of British work, and your task was to excite people about those commissions. You arranged five photo shoots for *Elle* with the five artists involved, including one of Bobby Baker hurling a pear across her kitchen into a wall for *Kitchen Show: One Dozen Kitchen Actions Made Public*. What did that achieve, do you think?

MB

You've got to seed the idea that something interesting is happening. And you seed that by choosing your publication. Basically, it's about trying to influence a group of people – not yet journalists and commissioning editors, that's the next stage. But with that project, you knew that if *Elle* was saying it, it became more likely that the *Guardian* might do something on it. Whereas, had I gone straight to the *Guardian*, there might have been a prejudice against covering it. So you go from stage to stage to stage, building and building.

That targeting process is essential. What happens now is that you get blanket coverage. In the old days, we sat at our desks with a pile of envelopes and a pile of press releases, and physically stuffed them in. So you would choose very carefully the people you'd address. Nowadays, the telephone and the email don't necessitate any selection process. You do too much, you contact too many people, and that's why we all get saturated and bored. In fact, all you need is one phone call to the right person at the right paper, and there'll be an explosion.

LN

New technologies can make the process harder. But they can also make it easier. I'm working on the Centenary Celebrations at the Tooting Bec Lido. Recently, two colleagues with an underwater camera took photographs of an artwork, at the bottom of the pool. Then they put the photograph on the image website Flickr, sent a press release out that afternoon, and the next day the picture and the whole press release was on the BBC website. I couldn't believe it: the whole thing, from conception to arriving on the BBC website in 24 hours. Totally DIY.

MB

It is exciting. With the democracy of the web and the reach of new communications technologies, it's incredible what you can achieve. And you can deploy more tools than ever to generate an audience for experimental work in particular. But if you go back to the principles of good publicity, they have not changed. The same methods were used by the promoters of the Roman forum through to Barnum and beyond. Everybody has curiosity. The technology is more sophisticated, but we're still driven by the same human emotions. Which goes back to what I said earlier: you have to be passionate, you have to believe. Nothing changes, really: contact and relationships remain.

BITE, Artsadmin and Duckie swap notes

Louise Jeffreys and Toni Racklin from the Barbican talk to Judith Knight of Artsadmin, Simon Casson from Duckie, and Daniel Brine of the Live Art Development Agency about BITE (Barbican International Theatre Events); its role in the theatre landscape, development of artists, and the changing nature of practice.

Bobby Baker, *How to Live*
Photo, Andrew Whittuck

The first BITE season was in 1998. It was the brainchild of the Barbican's Artistic Director Graham Sheffield and was informed by the Royal Shakespeare Company's decision not to continue to occupy the Barbican theatres all year-round, and research which identified that a gap in the London market was international theatre, particularly of a large scale.

By the end of the 1990s a lot of international work had been presented in London. We would never ever claim to be the first: LIFT was obviously extremely important, places like the Lyric Hammersmith frequently presented international work, and the National Theatre had international seasons. We benefited from situations that others made. But there hadn't been somewhere with a large stage that presented international work on such a regular basis and perhaps still isn't with the focus on performance that we have.

For BITE we have two theatres, the 1,100 seat main house and The Pit which is anything from about 100 – 180 seats depending on the formation. The context for these spaces is the arts centre, which also helps because alongside us we have cinemas, galleries and a concert hall, so there are opportunities on occasion for cross-fertilisation and festivals that take in all of those different spaces and genres.

Within our focus on large-scale international performance a lot of the work crosses boundaries and mixes genres, and we're not restricted by any particular box of dance or drama or music or anything, so we're completely free to look across every genre, and I think that is one of the situations that has been most important to us.

We do present British companies but what's absolutely true of the British companies we've presented is all of them have an international life. So it isn't the international companies *and* the British companies, it's the international companies of which some are British.

Similarly, in BITE we don't make distinctions between the different types of work we do – it isn't a case of 'oh we better take a risk on some experimental stuff.' We feel that we provide a theatre context in which experimental work can happen. But for us we just don't see a big difference between the most conservative work and the most experimental work that we do.

Judith Knight (JK)
One of the manifestations of your attitude is the BITE brochure, which seems to give equal weight to all productions, for instance Deborah Warner's *Julius Caesar* gets as much prominence as does something in The Pit. I think showing the work together in that context and demonstrating to your audiences that the programme is seen as a whole is incredibly important for both the smaller scale and the British work.

Toni Racklin (TR)
And that's very deliberate. It also reflects our own positioning, how we view our work. A show that comes in for half an hour in The Pit is as important and as valuable to us as a show that's going to run six weeks in the main house, because we all have to put the same amount of work into it – in administration, marketing, press – everything is of the same value and hopefully that is reflected in the brochure.

We always use our programmes and our website to say: 'well you're here for this, how about that? How about this one?' Where there are some parallels and some links into experimental work we very much want people to move out of what they would naturally come to and to see something else as well. People are trusting us – they'll look in the brochure, they'll see there's a multi-buy scheme and they'll book for shows they'd go to naturally and then also take in something else.

Daniel Brine (DB)
So, it is a long-term investment? Perhaps if Duckie's *C'est Barbican!* had been presented totally out of context and not built into a long-term plan, the audiences would not have come, and you are clearly interested in gaining the trust of audiences.

TR
We don't want a hit-and-run approach.

DB
And this implies developing relationships with companies as well as audiences?

LJ
Yes, and what works for us is when the artist or company and BITE both have a purpose. It has got to mean something to both of us. We have got to have a function and the artist or the company need to get something out of being here and when that comes together – which it often does by chance – then it really works.

TR
With Duckie it was actually synchronicity because we had been running a cabaret strand called *The Velvet Lounge* and then (as if by magic) we heard of this thing in this seedy pub in South London that I was so terrified to walk into that I had to be escorted in! And it was like ... 'oh yes this is it, of course, this is it.' And it was a marriage of the moment because it was a natural development for us and answered our remit, while at the same time Duckie had developed over many years and had a very strong following so it was a great chance to put strong work into a new context. So, we were transposing them here and

we made The Pit their home. It wasn't just plonking them in here, we had to create this environment that felt absolutely spot on, which was in itself a big ask. The next show we are doing together has a whole different set of challenges, for instance serving food within a show, and we have to address these things. We have to involve the box office, the front of house, the technical team, to ensure everyone at the Barbican embraces this and makes it a very smooth and very sharp operation.

Simon Casson (SC)

It was amazing how the audience changed when we came here – I've never seen so many straight people in my life all in one room together! And that's really interesting for us, so the audience became 50/50 straight/gay and it really burst us out of our bubble and our ghetto. For us, it was great.

JK

The same happened with Bobby Baker because she had performed a lot and had a huge following already before she came to the Barbican. Originally, she did The Pit for three weeks, and that built an audience. I knew by looking at the audience, and we do know from the Barbican's statistics, that many of the audience saw Bobby for the first time in The Pit. Bobby had always had a festival / visual arty / experimental theatre audience before – a LIFT audience – but after three weeks in The Pit there was an opportunity to present work on the main stage.

LJ

Because we realised there was a big and growing audience there, and that Bobby hadn't previously done a large-scale piece. So we tried Bobby on the main stage and that sold beyond all of our expectations. In fact, Duckie and Bobby Baker are two of the artists that we present that do very well at the box office – it's not a worry in that sense.

DB

So there's obviously fantastic benefits for the artist to come here, in terms of increasing audiences, but presumably there's a similar benefit for the Barbican in terms of introducing new audiences to the Barbican through these artists?

LJ

Absolutely! And expanding the reach of what we do.

DB

It's important to acknowledge that from the experimental theatre sector's point of view the absolutely important role the Barbican plays in presenting work to new audiences. There are some things that only a venue of the scale of the Barbican can do – such as extended runs or presenting work on larger stages. And it's very important in terms of the ecology of experimental practices that there are places like Duckie at the Vauxhall Tavern or Battersea Arts Centre (BAC) which can put on the first shows of practitioners working in more experimental ways. The artists can try out their ideas, they can develop them, then tour them around the country. Ultimately, there may be an opportunity to show the work in a venue like the Barbican but it's important to see the smaller experimental venues working in partnership. It might not be co-commissioning but in terms of the ecology it's a very important role that the Barbican plays.

LJ

And it's informal. Certainly with Ridiculusmus, the relationship with BAC and David Jubb has been extremely important. We began by presenting one of their works then we presented two together. Next time we'll hopefully present their films, do talks, panel discussions and present some of the older pieces as well so that we begin to have a critical focus on the work – something slightly different than just presenting.

SC

We should just be really clear about this, you're talking about performance that's experimental. Experimental performance by its very nature can fail. You can have a total flop. Because this is experimental theatre practice, some die on their arse and some are the most wonderful things you ever see.

DB

That's why a commitment from presenters to the long-haul is important. So that if something fails the next thing may not. It's also why different understandings of risk and nurturing risk are important. It's important that artists are able to develop their work out of the heat of the spotlight – that's the risk of the Duckies and BACs. Barbican's risk is very different, it is putting that type of work on this type of scale to this level of audience.

SC

And there are examples of how *not* to do it. One promoter put us on because the Barbican and the Sydney Opera House had put us on. You get this sense that some promoters or producers don't really know what they are dealing with! And they don't understand the need to think differently and perhaps creatively about all their business – from marketing to front of house. We did about 60 shows at the Barbican and every single one sold out, because they look after you and because they know what they are doing. But, you can't just put something on and cross your fingers, you need to know what you're dealing with and work to get it right.

DB

In a publication called *Towards 2010: New Times, New Challenges For The Arts,* Robert Hewison wrote that 'traditional buildings that present the arts will have to adapt to demands both from artists and audiences to rewrite their spaces.' Does this ring true for you – both the artist and the venues? And if so, what can 'adaptation' and 'rewriting' mean practically?

LJ

Well, I suppose we try and do it, which I think is the most important thing. I think there is still a real need for the umbrella organisations like Dance Umbrella and LIFT – those festival organisations which are not building-based and which say, quite rightly, that one of the benefits for them is that they can choose the right space for the right work. Our role is to work with the two spaces we have. Our production team bend over backwards from our constant demands; try and put a new auditorium in the main theatre, bring the main stage out, or change the seating in The Pit in a million different ways. Our job here is to programme these spaces and we try and be as flexible with them as we can but there's a limit beyond which we can't go.

JK

It's not just about getting theatres to take more risks, it is also about encouraging audiences to experience something new, and then to like it and in the end expect it. And it's not just about replacing the mainstream, it is more about infiltrating it, so that boundaries get narrower and experimental work is no longer put into a 'weird and wonderful' box, but is strong and leading the way, for everything else to follow.

DB

Hewison suggests that audiences are demanding a rewrite of our cultural spaces. Do you get a sense that audiences are seeking out different types of experiences which might go beyond the traditional theatrical spaces?

LJ

Absolutely, I think so, but the changing interests and attitudes of audiences are not matched in journalism and that's a huge problem. When we want someone to write about BITE, someone might write about the theatre, someone might write about the dance, someone might mention the operas we've done or music theatre. But whenever we try and think about someone who might write about all of BITE we find that very hard because newspapers have divided specialisms like opera, dance and theatre. In the *Observer* this week for Mark Morris' ENO production of *King Arthur* there was a big page and it used the word 'hybrid' but the dance critic had written about the dance part and in a box at the bottom the music critic had written about the music part – as if they were two completely different things! This needs to develop.

One development is that audiences are writing their own 'crits' on these new websites that are emerging. It's not big yet but I think it will be, and I think more and more people will want to write their own comments and let other people – other audiences – know about their experiences.

SC

And those experiences are important because they'll change your life. We'll remember them. I went to the Village Gate in New York in 1993 and saw Penny Arcade – they turned the lights out and Quentin Crisp spoke quietly and Marianne Faithful came on in-between the scenes singing the *Ballad of Lucy Jordan* and I had the time of my life! And I want to work with you lot and do that for other people. It's important to me.

DB

The changing of our lives, the activating of our lives – is there something that experimental work can do especially? Why would we invest in experimental work with all its difficulties and its challenges?

TR

Because it taps into new parts of us, and stretches us in new ways.

JK

Because it can change your way of thinking. It's imagination, it's looking at the world in a different way.

TR

You might know what you are going to get from a production of Shakespeare – however fine it is – it's kind of known but then something else – something new – can just shift you slightly.

LJ

It's that thought when you're seeing a show – even when you see shows as much as I do – 'my God I'd never have thought of that.' And that's that sort of wow moment when you see or think of something which has never struck you before. Those are the most exciting moments.

DB

Simon, didn't your marketing once say 'Demolish the Theatre', shouldn't the Barbican be scared of you?

SC

Well, I personally don't believe in The Theatre. I don't believe in the proscenium arch, I don't believe in the stalls. I want to take a baseball bat and smash them all up – I'm not interested in them, I'd set fire to them. I want to do something else. I just have this passion, and it's a lifelong passion and it's for performance – I call it performance. Now that touches on this thing called live art, it touches on this thing which is called theatre. I'd rather do it on the roof.

We are the modern world. We're not trying to understand someone else, we're fucking 'it'. I'm 40 this year, but I'm still 'it'. And the reason why I think this conversation is so important is because theatre needs to be revolutionary, ever-changing. Even bloody crappy telly ever-changes. Telly is very different now than it was ten years ago and performance culture has to change constantly too. That's why this notion of experimental in the mainstream isn't a question of 'should it happen?' But it's 'why isn't it happening and why isn't it happening faster?'

Making Smaller

Keith Khan talks to Lois Keidan of the Live Art Development Agency about his approaches as artistic director of the groundbreaking company motiroti, and his two years as CEO of London's Rich Mix.

Wearing your artist's hat, let's start by talking about the ways in which artists can influence audience development and the nature of cultural institutions. In particular, motiroti's *Moti Roti Puttli Chunni* (1993) at Theatre Royal Stratford East and the creation and touring of *Alladeen* (2003). How did the relationship with Theatre Royal begin?

After motiroti completed site-specific productions of *Flying Costumes, Floating Tombs* (1991) we were looking for a theatre venue for a new project that aimed to restage an Indian movie on stage, using all the tropes and facets of what happens in Bollywood. I was interested in the work of Philip Hedley, Artistic Director of Theatre Royal Stratford East, because he was very focused on audience development and had built an audience that was clearly not the kind of audience that other venues had. It seemed that the way Theatre Royal approached marketing and audience development was as important as their actual productions, and I thought that they would be a good fit for our own aspirations for this project. When I approached Philip Hedley, he not only agreed to house the project, but also to invest in it. The piece itself was a fairly conventional piece of narrative theatre – or rather it *looked* like a fairly conventional piece of narrative theatre – so it worked within Theatre Royal's structures. *Moti Roti Puttli Chunni* was a success and out of this we went on to do another piece with Theatre Royal, *One Night* (1997), but by then motiroti had dumped the conventional theatre model based on having the writer at the top of a hierarchy, and had instigated a much more collaborative model in which it was understood that the person doing the music, or the person doing the lighting, had as much to contribute to the creation of a theatre environment as anyone else involved.

motiroti and The Builders Association, *Alladeen*
Photo, Simone Lynn

LK

And how did that work for Theatre Royal? Was it a big shake-up for them to have to deal with the production of that kind of collaborative model?

KK

Well, it was all very different from what they normally did but they were really supportive and willing to take the risk. And of course they were committed to audience development and recognised that there weren't enough Asian audiences in the UK.

LK

So their strategy (as a venue and through their collaboration with you) was not about trying to persuade Asian audiences to come and see something they might not necessarily be interested in, but rather to try to create work that those audiences could be interested in.

KK

Exactly. It was about changing the programme and therefore changing the audience.

LK

I remember standing in the queue for *Moti Roti Puttli Chunni* at Theatre Royal and the man in front of me warning his friends that Keith Khan's work was 'a little bit weird'. I've always been intrigued as to whether he and his friends would have come to see the work if it hadn't been at Theatre Royal.

KK

I think the venue made a difference to the audiences we attracted. The other big difference was that Nitish Bharawaj who played Krishna in one of India's biggest soaps, *The Mahabarata*, was in the show. Working with someone who was not from a theatre background was great, because he brought with him a cinematic way of performing and acting that contributed enormously to the concept of the piece.

LK

So motiroti's strategy was about bringing together different approaches and practices and putting them together as something that 'looked like theatre' within a theatre.

KK

The strange thing is that we were absolutely committed to making *Moti Roti Puttli Chunni* in the way that Indian film was made – recreating in minute detail all of those effects like tracking shots and close-ups and the kind of interplay between screen and stage. I think that if we hadn't approached it so seriously and intensely it would have just been another piece of theatre.

LK

But it was still a fantastic night out *in* a theatre. One of the other things I remember from that night was that you had a great cliff-hanger before the interval where the murderer was revealed in Hindi but not English, so in the toilets during the interval there were all these women begging the Hindi speakers to tell them who the murderer was. This brought a dynamic to the theatre experience, and an energy to the venue, that I've rarely experienced.

KK

One of the things about the Theatre Royal audience is that they have a lot of energy, and are far from passive. But the touring of *Moti Roti Puttli Chunni* to theatres in the UK and internationally was horrible because the venues didn't have the same commitment to audience development and were not able to attract Asian audiences. Even if they did bring in different audiences, they often did not have the generosity or vision to

make those audiences feel welcome or comfortable. We had so
many conversations with venues in which we'd say: if people
come with their own food let them in, and if people come late let
them in because we don't mind, the cast don't mind and in fact
it'll benefit the show – a bit of rustling at the beginning is good.
But the venues were rarely interested in such conversations.

LK

So, Theatre Royal were able to break their own systems, to
accommodate different ways of working – both artistically
and with audiences – and other venues were resistant and that
showed in their audiences?

KK

Yes.

LK

Alladeen was a different model. It was a collaboration with The
Builders Association, an interdisciplinary theatre company from
New York, and was in many ways an even more conventional
piece of theatre.

KK

Ali Zaidi of motiroti and I had seen The Builders Association's
Jet Lag at the Barbican in London, which combined visual
narrative and cinematic imagery with theatre in ways I hadn't
seen before and so I proposed a collaboration to Marianne
Weems, the company's director and one of the leading theatre
and technology directors in the world. What's different about
the way that The Builders Association work is not only that
their pieces are more rooted in theatrical traditions but they also
involve co-producers at a very early stage. So from the outset
of our collaboration – even before we had a writer onboard –
there were four co-producers all of whom were taking risks and
making an investment in the piece: Barbican, London; Wexner

Centre, Columbus Ohio; Walker Arts Centre, Minneapolis; and
Museum of Contemporary Art, Chicago. The piece evolved
over a two-year period through workshop sessions supported
by the four initial co-producers and then we hired a space to try
out aspects of the piece and to invite other producing venues to
see where the work was at and to give us feedback. I think this
opening up of the process is a good way of working because
either further investment comes in or you realise that you
need to change the piece. I suppose you have to have sensitive
producers that appreciate seeing work at a fairly rough stage, but
for me to be actually directly collaborating with the venues from
such an early stage is a great model.

LK

The producers that you're talking about were venue managers,
not independent producers, and I imagine it is a really good
model for them as well. Possibly one of the challenges for venue
managers of such different ways of making theatre is that there
aren't necessarily any 'givens' – there isn't a script, and there
isn't a design you can look at to let you know how it's going to
work in your space. Because of the process-based way of making
experimental theatre it's difficult for venue managers to know
in advance what it will be like, and this makes it even more
high risk. But in the model you're proposing they are part of
the process: directly involved in the creation of the piece and
better equipped and informed to produce and promote the work
within their own distinct contexts.

KK

Yes, those rehearsals and development periods were really
crucial, and the input of those venues was important in terms of
moving the production on.

LK

I remember at the time you and Marianne Weems of The Builders Association saying that one of the things about the collaboration was that it was not just an artistic marriage but that it enabled The Builders Association to access your (Asian) audiences, and enabled motiroti to access white middle-class venues that would otherwise have been resistant. Did that work for both of you?

KK

Yes, it worked successfully all round. I think the door opening to the Barbican main house wouldn't have happened without The Builders Association. They helped the scaling up of the project and of motiroti, and likewise we helped broker the relationship with the Brooklyn Academy of Music which has ended up with them co-producing the company's next piece.

LK

Let's move on from motiroti to your taking on the role of Chief Executive Officer (CEO) of Rich Mix from 2004 to 2006. With that role you were wearing a very different hat but you still had the same cultural values. I would be interested in you talking about the ways in which you were positioning Rich Mix to be able to respond to notions of experimentation. How were you developing the building to meet the needs of new practices and new ways of working, and as somewhere that had a different set of cultural values from more rarefied and exclusive arts venues?

KK

It's very clear what my contribution to Rich Mix was: I created it as a house of process. Rich Mix has become a place where you can see work as it's being made and see artists trying things out. One of the things we instigated is the public studio with a window on to the street which will always have some kind of activity in it. My idea was to create an open cultural model that allows people in – that is about opening up process, about artists inviting people in to their work at different stages.

LK

And why do you think that's important?

KK

Well, because the first thing we tried was a static exhibition and I realised that it didn't really make sense for that building, or for its staff or even for the artists because the art seemed fossilised. Those tropes of the visual arts world are very powerful, but they didn't work in a new type of space as they are too passive. Coming to see this exhibition was a bit like going into a museum rather than a lively cultural place. On reflection what seemed to be important was when there were loads of kids and young men hanging around Leepu, the artist from Bangladesh we had invited to transform a non-status car into a super swish sports car. The audiences were actively engaging with what was going on, and we thought that maybe we didn't need passive pre-packaged exhibitions and could just invest in process itself.

But I was also looking at how outcomes and products from these processes can be packaged and produced and taken out of the building. I hoped that we might be able to evolve work at Rich Mix that would be of sufficient quality to end up on the main stage of the Barbican and in a way this follows the motiroti models.

I also think it is important for Rich Mix and other new cultural institutions to prioritise areas of culture that are less rarefied or restricted. So, I was not prioritising visual art because there are so many galleries in the East End of London and because we shouldn't be clogging up our spaces with the brokering of artists into galleries. Likewise with theatre. There are a lot of theatres out there and the work that Rich Mix presents should always be much more experimental, more risky, more politically engaged, and more concerned with audiences. So at Rich Mix we developed a set of Dogme-like rules – criteria by which we accept projects. We asked ourselves: Does it have political ramifications? Is it helping audience development? For us this was a really good way to think about how we develop both art for the future and audiences for the future.

LK

One of the exciting things about you, your work, and where you're heading is that you are looking at Culture rather than Art, and that you are blurring distinctions between restricted art and popular art, and setting different sorts of cultural values. And the fact that Rich Mix was not an existing building changing its artistic policy, but that you were starting it from scratch means that it could have the potential to be a unique and exciting model for the UK.

KK

Yes, I think it's a unique model. If you look around the world the models for new cultural institutions are limited because many of them are aimed at relatively minority markets and are preoccupied with economics – the visual arts world is certainly about economics and even the theatrical one to some degree. But there's a lot of important and exciting stuff happening that is on the one hand more experimental, and on the other, more accessible, and that is developing new cultural models, and there just aren't the kind of places for that. But having spent two years shaping that vision and creating local jobs at Rich Mix I've now moved on.

LK

Finally, can you talk about the importance of investing in different ways of working and the necessity of taking risks. Why shouldn't we play it safe?

There's a danger at the moment because audiences seem to be diminishing but actually they're just changing. Audiences have changed almost unrecognisably in the last ten years and the way that people engage with culture is fundamentally different now. The online component – the idea of user-generated content – is really critical now. The kind of public interface that technology gives means that even work that is 'minority' on a local level can reach 'majority' audiences globally who are interested in the same ideas. So, the future has got to be about making smaller and actually being more specialised, rather than becoming more generalist, because that's the kind of curse that we're seeing around us – a bland environment of safe culture, which is destined for mass appeal. I believe what's being missed is that if you invest in the edges you're going to end up with a much more vibrant fall out.

Programme Notes
Contributors' biographies

Marina Abramović is one of the seminal artists of our time. Since the early 1970s, when she attended the Academy of Fine Arts in Belgrade, she has pioneered the use of performance art as a visual art form. The body has always been both her subject and medium. Exploring the physical and mental limits of her being, she has withstood pain, exhaustion and danger in the quest for emotional and spiritual transformation. From 1975 to 1988, Marina and the German artist Ulay performed together, dealing with relations of duality. After separating in 1988, Marina has presented her work with performances, sound, photography, video and sculpture in solo exhibitions at major institutions in the US and Europe. In 1994, she became Professor for Performance Art at the Hochschule für Bildende Künste in Braunschweig, where she taught for seven years. In 2004, she was awarded an Honorary Doctorate from the Art Institute in Chicago. She was awarded the Golden Lion for Best Artist at the 1997 Venice Biennale for *Balkan Baroque*, and in 2003 received the Bessie for *The House with the Ocean View* at Sean Kelly Gallery, New York. In 2005,

she held a series of performances called *Seven Easy Pieces* at The Guggenheim Museum in New York, which was awarded the prize for 2005-2006 Best Exhibition of Time-Based Art by the United States Art Critics Association. In 2008, she was honored with the Austrian Commander Cross for her contributions to Art History, and in September 2009 decorated with the Honorary Doctorate of Arts by the University of Plymouth, UK. In 2010, she had her first major retrospective in the US at The Museum of Modern Art, New York, and simultaneously performed her durational piece *The Artist is Present* for more than 700 hours. In 2012, the HBO documentary, *The Artist is Present*, premiered at Sundance Film Festival in Utah.

Neil Bartlett is a director and author. His early work was as a performance artist. He has created work for venues and institutions as various as the ICA, the Drill Hall, the National Review of Live Art, the National Theatre, Artangel, the Royal Court, Battersea Arts Centre, the Derby Playhouse, the American Repertory Theatre, the Royal Shakespeare

Company, several derelict warehouses, almost every arts centre in the country, Southwark Cathedral and the Vauxhall Tavern. From 1994-2004, he was Artistic Director of the Lyric Hammersmith. Since leaving the Lyric, Neil has made work with and for the Manchester International Festival (three times), Handspring (at the National), the RSC, Opera North, the Barbican, The Brighton Festival (five times), Aldeburgh and The Abbey in Dublin, where he recently sold out a nine-week mainhouse run of his new take on Wilde's *The Picture of Dorian Gray*. He has also, he is proud to say, been back to the Vauxhall Tavern a few times. www.neil-bartlett.com

Mark Borkowski is a publicity consultant, author and thinker who helps brands to discover and retool their narratives for traction in the Now Economy. He's worked with a huge roster of brands and figures, from multinational corporations to politicians to underground circuses.

Mary Brennan is the dance and performance critic for *The Herald* newspaper, Scotland's leading quality broadsheet. She also writes about children's theatre, and is a member of the CATS (Critics' Awards for Theatre in Scotland) panel. She reviewed National Theatre of Scotland's *Home East Lothian* in 2006 and still remembers the raw

intensity of following Hansel and Gretel through a dank, scary night-time wood towards the welcoming lights of the witch's house. More recently, she watched NTS perform a lo-tech eco-friendly production of *The Last Polar Bear* to a small gathering of primary-school pupils in the East Ayrshire village of Sorn. The youngsters were utterly smitten – not least when the cast packed everything into wee trailers behind their bikes and cycled off to the next community gig.

Simon Casson is the producer for Duckie, a post-gay performance and events collective that create good nights out. Duckie make event culture: audience interactive experiences that blur the boundaries between theatre, nightclubs and arty show business. From their legendary 17-year residency at the Royal Vauxhall Tavern to winning Olivier awards at the Barbican, these pony purveyors of progressive working-class entertainment mix live art and light entertainment. Duckie see themselves in a tradition of British Illegitimate theatre that spans centuries – from music hall to punk rock, penny gaffs to the fairground. duckie.co.uk

Amanda Coogan is a performance artist living in Dublin, Ireland. The centrality of Coogan's practice is durational live performance where

powerful live events are fundamental to her videos and photographs. Her expertise lies in her ability to condense an idea to its very essence and communicate it through her body. Coogan was awarded the Allied Irish Bank's Art prize in 2004. She performs and exhibits her work widely including Dublin Contemporary 2011, The Whitworth Gallery, Manchester, The Museum of Fine Arts, Boston, Artists Space, New York, The Venice Biennale 03, Liverpool Biennial 04, PS1, New York, The Irish Museum of Modern Art, Royal Hibernian Academy, Van Gogh Museum, Amsterdam, Trace Gallery, Cardiff and Limerick City Gallery of Art.
www.amandacoogan.com

Tim Etchells is an artist and a writer based in the UK whose work shifts between performance, visual art and fiction. He has worked in a wide variety of contexts, notably as the leader of the world-renowned performance group Forced Entertainment. In recent years he has exhibited widely in the context of visual arts, participating in biennales Manifesta 7 (2008) in Rovereto, Italy, Art Sheffield 2008, Goteborg Bienale (2009), October Salon Belgrade (2010), Aichi Trienale, Japan 2010, with Vlatka Horvat and Manifesta 9 (Parallel Projects) 2012. He has had solo shows at Gasworks and Sketch (London), Bunkier Sztuki

(Krakow) and Künstlerhaus Bremen. Etchells' first novel *The Broken World* was published by Heinemann in 2008 and his monograph on contemporary performance and Forced Entertainment, *Certain Fragments* (Routledge, 1999), is widely acclaimed. A publication based on his 2011 online project *Vacuum Days* was published by Storythings in October 2012. Tim Etchells is Professor of Performance at Lancaster University.
www.timetchells.com
www.forcedentertainment.com

Vicky Featherstone is founding Artistic Director and Chief Executive of the National Theatre of Scotland. She left the Company in December 2012 to become Artistic Director of the Royal Court Theatre, London. Productions for the Company include: *Appointment with The Wicker Man* by Greg Hemphill and Donald McLeary, *Enquirer* (co-directed with John Tiffany), *27* by Abi Morgan, *The Wheel* by Zinnie Harris, *Somersaults* by Iain Finlay MacLeod, *Wall of Death: A Way of Life* (co-directed with Stephen Skrynka), *The Miracle Man* by Douglas Maxwell, *Empty* by Cathy Forde, *Long Gone Lonesome* by Duncan McLean, *Cockroach* by Sam Holcroft, *365* by David Harrower, *Mary Stuart* and *The Wolves In The Walls* (co-directed with Julian Crouch).
www.nationaltheatrescotland.com

Matt Fenton is Director of Live at LICA (Lancaster Institute for the Contemporary Arts). The organisation combines three important arts venues – Nuffield Theatre Lancaster, Peter Scott Gallery and Lancaster International Concerts – and operates at the intersection of contemporary practice, academic research and public engagement. Matt is a practising theatre director and dramaturg, and also teaches on Lancaster University's Masters programme in Contemporary Arts Practice, a course he developed in response to the needs of early career artists.
www.liveatlica.org

Rose Fenton is the Director of Free Word, London, the UK's first dedicated centre for literature, literacy and free expression. She is co-Founder with Lucy Neal of the London International Festival of Theatre (LIFT) and was its Co-Director for 25 years. Rose has worked as a freelance producer and arts adviser, leading projects with, amongst others, FIT – Festivals in Transition – an initiative by eight European festivals to develop the role of international theatre festivals within the cultural landscape of an evolving Europe. Rose is on the board of Dance Umbrella and Aerowaves, and Chair of Without Walls, a consortium of leading UK Festivals collaborating to produce groundbreaking performance in outdoor spaces. In 2005, Rose was awarded an OBE for Services to Drama. She holds an Honorary Doctorate from De Montford University and an Honorary Fellowship from Dartington College of Arts. Her book, *The Turning World: Stories from the London International Festival of Theatre*, co-written with Lucy Neal, was published in 2005.
www.freewordonline.com

Andy Field is the co-director of Forest Fringe. "I am an artist, writer, part-time curator, sometime academic and very occasional performer who lives in Bristol but works all over the place. I am interested in adventurous and unusual work whether it calls itself theatre, live art, performance, installation, sound art or anything else. My own work is diverse, slipping between disciplines as a means of exploring a preoccupation with cities, everyday performance, trashy films, radical politics and what it feels like to be around at this strange moment in time. In addition to co-directing Forest Fringe I'm also Associate Artist/Producer at Arnolfini". @andytfield
www.forestfringe.co.uk

Lyn Gardner writes about theatre for the *Guardian*. Her latest series of novels for children is published by Nosy Crow.

Stella Hall is a freelance Festival and Events consultant with a passion for bringing people and place together through shared creative experiences. Her early work included co-founding the Green Room, Manchester and she has since worked in a number of high-profile roles including Festival Director, Belfast Festival at Queens and Creative Director, culture 10, the innovative programme of festivals and events across NE England which ran until 2009. Most recently she became the first ever Festival Director of Preston Guild 2012, an event occurring in the city every twenty years since 1179 and for which she was made an Honorary Fellow of University of Central Lancashire. She is a Board member of Wildworks, Cornwall, and Artsadmin, London and a member of the REF (Research Excellence Framework) 2014 panel for Drama, Dance, Music and Performing Arts.

Louise Jeffreys was previously Head of Theatre and Arts Projects and has worked for the Barbican Centre since 1999. Prior to the Barbican, previous roles include Administrative Director at the Nottingham Playhouse, Head of Production at Bayerische Staatsoper, Munich, and Technical Director at the English National Opera.
www.barbican.org.uk

David Jubb became Artistic Director of BAC in 2004. Prior to that he was Director of Your Imagination (2001-2004), a company dedicated to producing independent artists including Ridiculusmus and Toby Jones. He worked as Producer at BAC with Artistic Director Tom Morris (1999-2001); was Director of the Lion & Unicorn Theatre for Central School of Speech and Drama (1998-1999) and worked as a teacher and lecturer in secondary and higher education. He is currently Chair of Kneehigh Theatre and the London Theatre Consortium.
www.bac.org.uk

Keith Khan is a designer and artist. He is also a cultural leader with expertise in policy/strategy. Keith's roles have included Head of Culture to London 2012, Chief Executive of Rich Mix (a multi-million pound new-build arts venue in East London, which he opened in 2004), Artistic Director for the Queen's Golden Jubilee Commonwealth Parade, and Director of Design Ceremonies for the Manchester Commonwealth Games. He was also co-Founder and Artistic Director of the arts organisation motiroti (1999-2004). His award-winning arts projects include *Alladeen, Escapade* and

Moti Roti Puttli Chunni. Keith runs Keith Khan Associates, London-based, with international reach. The company focus is on design and technology, and launched in Mumbai as part of India Design Week. It produced the Olympic celebrations for London Borough of Hackney; Brought Rio carnival for the London Olympics; delivered *L'île de Londres*, a weekend of Londoness with a twist for Lille 3000; and was creative lead for *Carnival Crossroads* for the UK Centre for Carnival Arts. The company is currently advising the Aga Khan Foundation on their capital plans for a new cultural building for London. Keith's artistic skills and new approaches to engaging a non-traditional arts audience have enabled him to serve as a member of National Council of Arts Council of England, and the Commonwealth Group on Culture and Development. www.keithkhanassociates.com

Judith Knight is the founder and co-Director of Artsadmin which for 33 years has produced, developed and supported experimental and interdisciplinary arts projects. It established Toynbee Studios as a centre for the development of new work, with an advisory and bursary scheme, residencies, an education programme and regular showcases and performances. Artsadmin produces the work of many artists whose work is presented locally, nationally and internationally. www.artsadmin.co.uk

Brian Logan is an arts writer for the *Guardian*, former assistant theatre editor of Time Out London, and writes regularly for the *Independent on Sunday*, the *New Statesman*, *The Times* and elsewhere. He is co-director of Camden People's Theatre, a London venue dedicated to adventurous performance from emerging artists. Brian is also a founder member of the touring theatre company Cartoon de Salvo, with whom he has devised and performed in 11 major shows, including *Meat & Two Veg* (BAC and international tour), *The Sunflower Plot*, *Hard Hearted Hannah and Other Stories* (Lyric Hammersmith, Edinburgh Fringe and Kennedy Center, Washington DC) and *Pub Rock*. Brian is also a freelance director and playwright.

John E McGrath is the founding Artistic Director of National Theatre Wales, where he has worked with a wide range of artists and partner companies to develop an award-winning mix of work in theatres and site-specific locations across the country. For National Theatre Wales he has directed *A Good Night Out in the Valleys* by Alan Harris (in five Valleys Miners' Institutes), *Love Steals Us From Loneliness* by Gary

Owen (staged in a Bridgend rock club), *The Radicalisation of Bradley Manning* by Tim Price (with every show live-streamed and hyperlinked online) and *In Water I'm Weightless* by Kaite O'Reilly (at the Wales Millennium Centre and South Bank Centre) as part of the 2012 Festival, the Finale of the Cultural Olympiad. John has also worked as a theatre director in New York, London and Manchester. From 1999-2008 he was Artistic Director of Contact, Manchester. He has published a book about art in the surveillance age, *Loving Big Brother: Performance, Privacy and Surveillance Space*, and in 2005 was awarded the National Endowment for Science Technology and the Arts (NESTA) Cultural Leadership Award. nationaltheatrewales.org

David Micklem was appointed Joint Artistic Director of BAC in April 2008, having joined the company as Executive Director in 2007. Prior to that he was Senior Theatre Officer at Arts Council England (2000-2007). During that time he was also Associate Producer for Artichoke on *The Sultan's Elephant* and commissioned *The Producers: Alchemists of the Impossible* in collaboration with The Jerwood Foundation. Prior to that he was General Manager of the Chelsea Theatre (1995-2000); and worked extensively as a freelance producer.

He is currently Chair of Wildworks and a Trustee of Artichoke Productions.
www.bac.org.uk

Lucy Neal is interested in the art of social sculpture and how celebratory events act as a catalyst for change. Co-founding director of the LIFT Festival, recent projects, Emergence The Summit at the Centre for Alternative Technology and the Tooting Transition Shop, explore the role of the arts in the shift to a more ecological and life sustaining society. Co-author of MMM's *Sustainable Ability* (www.sustainableability. com), she is Happiness Associate on the Happy Museum Project (www. happymuseumproject. org) and co-founder of Case For Optimism. (www.Caseforoptimism. co.uk). Active in the Transition Town movement since 2008, she is currently writing *Playing For Time*, the Transition Book on the Arts. She was awarded an OBE in 2005 for Services to Drama.

Deborah Pearson is founder and co-director of multi-award-winning artist-led Forest Fringe. Her work explores narrative in contemporary performance, a topic she is researching for a practice based PhD at Royal Holloway. Her 2010 solo piece *Like You Were Before* won a Herald Angel and was shortlisted for the Total Theatre Award for

Innovation. Her most recent piece, *The Future Show*, is a continually rewritten account of her future from the end of the show until the end of her life.
www.forestfringe.co.uk

Alex Poots is the founding director of the Manchester International Festival (MIF). He was appointed Festival Director in January 2005, conceiving and establishing MIF as an artist-led, commissioning festival presenting new works from across the spectrum of performing arts, visual arts and popular culture. Highlights of the first three Festivals include: Chinese opera *Monkey: Journey to the West*, group art event *Il Tempo del Postino*, *It Felt Like a Kiss* by Punchdrunk and Adam Curtis, Zaha Hadid Architects' new space for the music of Bach, Björk's *Biophilia* live show and Robert Wilson's *The Life and Death of Marina Abramović*. Before MIF, Alex commissioned, curated and presented new work and special events for the Barbican, Tate, Somerset House, Channel 4 and ENO, working with artists including PJ Harvey, Anish Kapoor, Ennio Morricone, Peter Sellars, Karlheinz Stockhausen, Steve McQueen and Sir John Eliot Gardiner. In addition to his role as Festival Director of Manchester International Festival, Alex was appointed Artistic Director of New York's Park Avenue Armory in December 2011. This new role will also facilitate a co-commissioning partnership between MIF and the Armory.
www.mif.co.uk

Toni Racklin joined the Barbican Centre in 1996 as Administrative Producer to launch BITE (Barbican International Theatre Events), the yearly programme of distinctive dance, drama and music theatre from around the world. Before joining the Barbican, she worked with a diverse range of companies including the Roundhouse, the Royal Court, Lyric Hammersmith, Womens Playhouse Trust, Liverpool Playhouse and Festival d'Aix en Provence. In October 2010, Toni was appointed Head of Theatre at the Barbican.
www.barbican.org.uk

Alan Rivett is Director of Warwick Arts Centre, the largest multidisciplinary venue in the UK outside London, based on the campus of University of Warwick in Coventry. Since being appointed in 2001 he has successfully steered Warwick Arts Centre's programme to a position where it regularly hosts high-profile, contemporary, international theatre, music, visual arts and interdisciplinary events. Warwick Arts Centre regularly commissions new work from leading artists and has a generative programme for emerging artists.

Alan is Chair of Fierce Festival Ltd, leading an annual festival of contemporary live art and performance in Birmingham and the West Midlands. He also Chairs the UK-wide Dance Touring Partnership, comprising leading UK venues committed to promoting international contemporary dance. Alan is also a board member of Shared Experience Theatre Company and The British Association of Concert Halls and has just completed a six-year term as a Council member of the University of Warwick. www.warwickartscentre.co.uk

Credits

ited by Lois Keidan and CJ Mitchell

st published in 2013 by

e Art Development Agency
e White Building
it 7, Queen's Yard
ite Post Lane
ndon E9 5EN
ww.thisisLiveArt.co.uk

d

eron Books Ltd
Caledonian Road
ndon N7 9RH
ww.oberonbooks.com

ntributions © individual contributors.

quotations taken from the first edition of
ogramme Notes, 2007, and reproduced with thanks.

ver image: *Empty Stages: Ghent*. Photo, Hugo
endinning and Tim Etchells.

photographs and photograph credits generously
ovided by contributors.

signed by David Caines Unlimited
ww.davidcaines.co.uk

3N: 978-1-84943-459-1

th thanks to all the contributors, Harriet Curtis,
go Glendinning, Neil Darlison and Jonny Hey
Arts Council England.

e first edition of *Programme Notes* (2007) was
-edited by Daniel Brine (now the Director
Cambridge Junction). We thank him for
at important work, which is still central to
s collection.

The Live Art Development Agency (LADA)

LADA offers Resources, Professional Development
Initiatives, and Projects & Publishing for the support
and development of Live Art artists, audiences and
discourses in the UK and internationally. LADA
works strategically, in partnership and in consultation
with artists and organisations in the cultural sector
and is committed to creating the conditions in which
diversity, experimentation and risk can thrive.

Oberon Books

Visit www.oberonbooks.com to read more about
all our books and to buy them. You will also find
features, author interviews and news of any author
events, and you can sign up for e-newsletters so that
you're always first to hear about our new releases.

Financially assisted by Arts Council England.

e Art
velopment
ency

Supported using public funding by
ARTS COUNCIL
ENGLAND

Martin Freeman as Buttons in *Cinderella*,
devised by Improbable Theatre with Neil Bartlett
Lyric Hammersmith, 1999
Photo, John Haynes

www.ingramcontent.com/pod-product-compliance
Ingram Content Group UK Ltd.
Pitfield, Milton Keynes, MK11 3LW, UK
UKHW022130020325
455697UK00009B/126

9 781849 434591